TIME TRAILS

RadioTimes

TIME TRAILS

Pathways through the Past

in association with

ENGLISH HERITAGE

CADW
WELSH HISTORIC MONUMENTS

ENVIRONMENT
AND HERITAGE
SERVICE

Published 2000 by *Radio Times*,
BBC Worldwide Ltd,
80 Wood Lane,
London W12 0TT

Project Managers:
Elizabeth Ollier
Tina Stevens
Cover design: Trish Bricusse
Cover photograph: Rievaulx Abbey, Yorkshire. © Pictor International

Designed and produced for *Radio Times* by

Creative Imprint

16 Rankine House
Port Dundas Business Park
Glasgow G4 9XG

Printed and bound by Oriental Press, Dubai

Contents

Contents

Please note that the trails in Scotland, Wales and Northern Ireland are over longer distances and are therefore all designed as drives rather than walks.

Kirkwall
p124

0   50 miles
0   50 kilometres

Indicates starting point
of each trail and relevant
page number

p126 •Aberdeen

SCOTLAND

•Dundee

p120 p122
Glasgow •
Edinburgh
p118

Berwick-upon-Tweed
p24
p26

NORTH
EAST
ENGLAND

p32

Bushmills
p134
•Londonderry

p30 •Newcastle upon Tyne

NORTHERN
IRELAND

Carlisle p18
p16
Penrith

p28

•Middlesborough

•Belfast

p36

p136
Armagh

p14 p20

p44

p38

NORTH
YORKSHIRE
AND THE HUMBER

p40

Barrow in
Furness

NORTH
WEST
ENGLAND

•York

•Kingston-upon-Hull

Leeds•

•Conwy
p132
Caernarfon•

Manchester•

p42

Chester p54
p12 p50

Lincoln
p56

MIDLANDS

Norwich
p76

Shrewsbury•

•Leicester

King's Lynn•

p64 p60

Great Yarmouth

WALES

Birmingham•

p58

p48

EAST
ENGLAND

p72

p130

Hereford•

p66

p52

p78

p62

p70

Ipswich

p114

p74

Pembroke•

p128 Gloucester•

LONDON

Chepstow•

p84-90

Cardiff•

Bath•

p82

p100

Bristol•

SOUTH EAST ENGLAND

p96
•Dover

p106

SOUTH WEST ENGLAND

p98

p94

Southampton•

Brighton•

Eastbourne

p112 Exeter•

p102

p108

•Plymouth

Penzance• p110

Pathways through the Past

The number of TV and radio programmes made recently about history suggests that the public's thirst for the subject has never been greater. This is why *Radio Times* has teamed up with English Heritage to create this fascinating and informative book. At the very least, it's a collection of great days out in some of Britain's most beautiful places. Used to its full potential, it offers a truly enriching insight into our nation's regional history, from the coastal splendour of Arthurian Cornwall to the dry-stone towers of prehistoric Orkney. Moreover, the contributions from our nine radio and TV celebrities add a personal touch to these exciting journeys into the past.

Whether you keep it in your bookcase, your rucksack or your car, the *Radio Times Time Trails* book is a unique guide to getting out and enjoying the extraordinary richness of our heritage and landscape.

Radio Times would like to take this opportunity to thank English Heritage for the use of its superb text and pictures on the English trails. Thank you also to Historic Scotland, CADW and Environment and Heritage Service, Northern Ireland for their guidance in compiling the Scottish, Welsh and Northern Irish trails.

Loyd Grossman

I made my first trip to the North West in 1975 because I wanted to see the Walker Art Gallery and visit Manchester Town Hall. The Walker was familiar from many credits in art-history books and my love of Victorian revivalist architecture (in this case Gothic) meant that I had studied Alfred Waterhouse's Town Hall long before I ever got to walk through the front door of the real thing. And that's how a love affair with the region began that has now gone on for nearly 25 years. Every subsequent trip unfolded a new layer of history or beauty.

The North West is an incredibly varied region whose extremes of topography and landscape are reflected in a built heritage that ranges from Hadrian's Wall to the dense urban development of the industrial revolution. **Barrow-in-Furness** is a great example of what the North West has to offer: the moody and powerful ruins of a glorious Cistercian abbey are just a brief trip away from the Victorian engineering work of the **Graving Dock** and the **Dock Museum.**

In the North West you'll find market towns, mills, museums and even a glimpse into outer space. Every visit I make to the North West – and fortunately they are frequent – shows me just how much more there is to discover, to learn and to enjoy there.

Right: Sunset over Hadrian's Wall.

Cheshire time
TRAVELS

Length: About 70 miles, one/two days

Starting point: Market Square, Sandbach

For a giant leap in time and space, take a few steps to see Jodrell Bank Observatory, 4,000 year old weaponry and 150 years of railway history at Crewe.

The Sandbach Crosses **1** are rare Saxon crosses from the ninth century, carved with animals, dragons and biblical scenes. Look out for other interesting buildings near to the Market Square. Lower Chequer Inn is the oldest building in town, built 1570. The Old Hall, High Street was built in 1656 and the Black Bear Inn, the Market Tavern and The Crown are all 17th century.

Crewe **2** is for all railway enthusiasts! The Centre has huge collections to explore. **Nantwich 3** is a charming market town set beside the River Weaver. It has a wealth of beautiful, old, timber-framed buildings, a wide range of shops, one of the finest medieval town churches in Britain and an interesting museum. Eleven miles south east of Chester off the A49 or A41 is **Beeston Castle 4**, built from 1226 and soon to

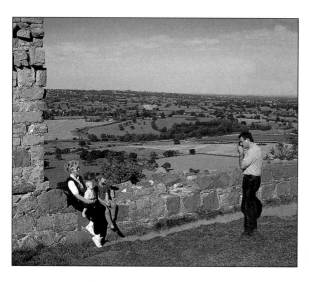

Left: Beeston Castle.
Bottom Left: Sandbach Crosses.

Jodrell Bank.

become a royal stronghold, only falling centuries later during the Civil War. **Delamere Forest** ⑤ is route-marked with forest walks, cycle trails and a route for disabled visitors. The visitor centre will help you with more information about the flora and fauna.

A mile from Northwich town centre is **Marbury Country Park and Mere**. ⑥ Dating from the early 13th century, the park was extensively re-planted in the 1840s. The present park extends to 220 acres and includes the third largest mere (lake) in Cheshire, where rare migrant birds can often be seen. There is good disabled access to the bird hide.

Take the M6 Junction 19 into Knutsford on A5033 and you will find **Tabley House** ⑦ the finest Palladian mansion in the north-west of England – now Grade I listed. The present building was completed in 1760 to a design by John Carr of York, but has been the seat of the Leicester family from 1272. Look out for the folly in the surrounding park. Near Holmes Chapel on A535 (Junction 18 off M6) is **Jodrell Bank** ⑧, the second largest steerable radio telescope in the world, constructed in 1957 and now a listed historic building.

OPENING TIMES

Sandbach Crosses (English Heritage), open at any reasonable time. **01244 602666.** Free entry.

The Railway Age, Vernon Way, Crewe, open daily 10am-4pm (Feb-Oct). **01270 212130.** Admission charge.

Nantwich Tourist Information Centre. Information on **01270 610983.**

Beeston Castle (English Heritage), open daily 10am-6pm (April-Sept), 10am-5pm (Oct), 10am-4pm (Nov-March). Closed 24-26 Dec and 1 Jan. **01829 260464.** Admission charge.

Delamere Forest (Forestry Commission), open daily all year 10.30am-4.30pm. Closed 25 Dec. Information on **01606 882167.**

Marbury Country Park (Cheshire County Council), open daily 9am-8pm (May-Sept), 9am-5pm (Oct-April). Information on **01606 77741.**

Tabley House (University of Manchester), open Thurs-Sun and Bank Hols (April-Oct). **01565 750151.** Admission charge.

Jodrell Bank (University of Manchester), open 11am-4.30pm Tues-Sun. **01477 571339.** Admission charge.

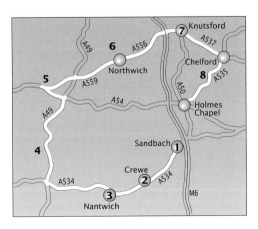

North west
MILLS

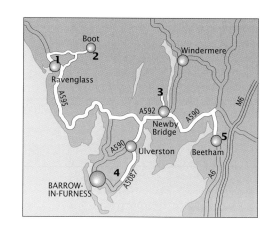

Length: About 50 miles, one/two days

Starting point: Ravenglass, Cumbria

Fancy 'milling' about? Then visit Stott Park Bobbin Mill, Muncaster Watermill and Eskdale Mill and others for a glimpse into the working life of today's mills.

Off the A595, one mile NE of Ravenglass is **Muncaster Mill** ❶. Trains of the Ravenglass and Eskdale Narrow Gauge Railway (L'al Ratty) stop at the mill station by request. This was once a manorial mill for Muncaster Castle on a site occupied since before 1455. The present building dates from about 1700 and the machinery is mostly pre-1850. The 13ft diameter overshot waterwheel powers, via a layshaft drive, three pairs of millstones and other machinery. There is also a drying kiln. The leat supplying the water from the River Mite is $3/4$ miles long. Organic wheat is ground to produce a wide range of flour for sale in the mill shop.

  Eskdale Mill ❷, Boot Village, is one of the oldest working mills in England. Eskdale Mill's two overshot wheels are driven by Whillan Beck as it tumbles down spectacularly from Sca Fell. All the original machinery for grinding oatmeal is in full working order and operated daily. Boot Village is a short walk from Dalegarth station, inland terminus of the famous Ravenglass and Eskdale steam railway or you can visit by car over the exhilarating Hardknott Pass. **Stott Park Bobbin Mill** ❸ was built in 1835 and is preserved as a working museum. It is typical of the mills of

Bobbins at Stott Park Bobbin Mill.

the Lake District that supplied bobbins to the spinning and weaving industry in Lancashire and demonstrates the bobbin-making machinery and techniques of the 19th century. It was powered by a static steam engine in tandem with a water turbine. Follow signs from the A5087 into the country lanes of rural Cumbria and you will reach **Gleaston Watermill 4**. The present buildings date from 1774, with original wooden gearing from the 1700s. Milling machinery and the 18ft waterwheel operate most days.

The Heron Corn Mill 5 is at Beetham. The present building dates from around 1740, with some contemporary machinery. The waterwheel is driven by water taken from the River Bela.

Stott Park Bobbin Mill.

OPENING TIMES

Muncaster Mill, Ravenglass, open daily 10am-5pm (Easter-Oct), 11am-3pm weekends (Nov-March). **01229 717232** Admission charge.

Eskdale Mill, Boot Village, open daily except Mon 11am-5pm (April-Oct). **019467 23335**. Admission charge.

Stott Park Bobbin Mill (English Heritage), open daily 10am-6pm (April-Sept), 10am-5pm (Oct). Closed Nov-March. **01539 531087**. Admission charge.

Gleaston Watermill, open daily 11am-5pm (Easter-Oct), 11am-4pm weekends only in winter. **01229 869244**.

Heron Corn Mill, Beetham, open daily 11am-5pm (April-Sept) except Mon (open Bank Holiday). **015395 65027**.

'Cup and ring' decoration from Maughanby, c2000-1500BC (Penrith Museum).

A **perambulation** around **PENRITH**

Length: About 36 miles, one/two days

Starting point: Middlegate, Penrith

Investigate this charming historic market town with a trail that includes a museum, two castles, prehistoric stones and churches.

Begin the trail at **Penrith Museum** 1 and find out about the area's fascinating past. The museum is located in a 300-year-old school which is next to the Penrith Tourist Information Centre. 14th-century **Penrith Castle** 2 is set in a park on the edge of the town opposite the railway station. The castle was begun in 1399 when William Strickland, later to become Bishop of Carlisle and Archbishop of Canterbury, added a stone

wall to the earlier pele tower. The castle was improved and added to over the next 70 years, becoming a Royal fortress for Richard, Duke of Gloucester. Travel south from Penrith and **Brougham Castle** 3 is on a minor road off the A66. The impressive ruins of the castle on the bank of the River Eamont include an early 13th-century keep and later buildings. Its one-time owner Lady Anne Clifford restored the castle in the 17th century. At Eamont Bridge, one mile south of Penrith is **Arthur's Round Table** 4, a prehistoric circular earthwork bounded by a ditch and an outer bank.

Close by is the **Mayburgh Earthwork** 5, an impressive prehistoric circular earthwork, with banks up to 15ft high, enclosing a central area of $1^1/_2$ acres containing a single large stone. From Eamont Bridge, travel south towards Kendal for about one mile. Take a left turn to Cliburn and **Wetheriggs** 6 is $1^1/_2$ miles along this road on the right hand side. There has been a working pottery at Wetheriggs since 1855 and it is the only surviving steam-powered country pottery in the British Isles. From Long Marton Church, take the junction before the church which leads back to the A66. Turn right and head for Penrith. Turn right on to the B6412 towards Culgaith. Continue on this road to Langwathby, turn left and then right for

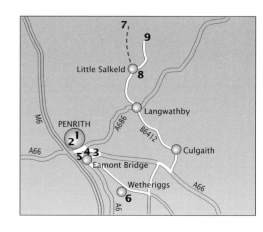

Left: Brougham Castle.
Below: Long Meg and Her Daughters.
(Eden Tourism)

OPENING
TIMES

Penrith Museum, open 10am-5pm Mon-Sat, 1pm-5pm Sun (April-Oct). **01768 212228**. Free entry.

Penrith Castle (English Heritage), park open daily 7.30am-9pm, winter 7.30am-4.30pm. Free entry.

Brougham Castle (English Heritage), open daily 10am-6pm (April-Sept), 10am-5pm (Oct). Closed Nov-March. **01768 862488**. Admission charge.

Arthur's Round Table & Mayburgh Earthwork (English Heritage), open at any reasonable time. Free entry.

Wetheriggs Pottery, open daily 10am-5pm all year except for Christmas and 1 Jan. **01768 892733**. Free entry.

Little Salkeld Watermill, open for tours 10.30am-5pm Mon, Tues, Thurs 10.30am-5pm (March-Oct). **01768 881523**. Admission charge.

Little Salkeld where you will find **Lacy's Caves** (7) after a pleasant walk of about $1^1/_2$ miles beside the River Eden. Lacy's Caves, carved out of soft red sandstone above the swirling waters of the mature River Eden, are amazing and enigmatic structures. The caves are an 18th-century folly on a grand scale and were probably carved by Colonel Lacy's workmen from nearby Salkeld Hall. To complete the illusion the Colonel employed a hermit to live in the caves.

Little Salkeld Watermill (8) is a delightful 18th-century country cornmill, still producing organic stoneground flour the traditional way. Continue on the road from Little Salkeld towards Glassonby. After a short distance **Long Meg** (9) is signposted down a narrow lane on the left. The 68 or so stones make Long Meg (and her daughters, so legend has it!) one of the largest prehistoric stone circles in the country. Retrace your steps to Langwathby where a right turn onto the A686 will take you back to Penrith.

The city of
CARLISLE

Length: At least one day

Starting point: Old Town Hall

Forget Milan, Carlisle produces tweeds for the international fashion market. Forget the Wild West, Carlisle had its own outlaws!

Dating from 1682, the **Carlisle or Carel Cross** ❶ was once a traditional meeting place in the city. Public proclamations were made from this cross. It was from here in 1745, at the time of the Jacobite Rising, that Bonnie Prince Charlie claimed the throne for his father. The lion on top of the cross holds the 'Dormont Book' (dated 1561) which contains a list of byelaws and lists of apprenticeships. Looking beyond the Old Town Hall, the three-storey timber framed building on the corner of this building is the **Guildhall**, ❷ also known as Redness Hall and dating from the 15th century. The Guildhall was once the meeting place of the City's trade guilds, but is now a museum. Continue from the Guildhall across the pedestrianised city centre and down St Cuthbert's Lane.

At the end of the lane is **St Cuthbert's Church** ❸. The church dates from 1778 and contains a 14th-century window (from an earlier church) set in the north wall. The interior has a gallery supported by Tuscan columns and a unique 'moveable' pulpit (around 1900) mounted on rails. On the far right side of the churchyard is the **15th-century Tithe Barn** ❹. It was here that the church collected a 'tithe'. Return back through the churchyard and turn right, continue the trail by turning right into

Heads Lane, passing The Sportsman Inn where, roughly opposite the Tithe Barn on the West Walls, are the **Sallyport Steps** ❺. The steps lead from the Sally Port, which was one of a number of secret gateways in the wall used when the city was under siege. Later, locals used the steps to get goods to the Tithe Barn without paying tolls at the city gates.

Carlisle's city walls were built between 1122 and 1200. **The West Walls** ❻ are a fine example of what a medieval walled city looked like. Continue down the steps and follow the path along the foot of the wall to view the impressive masonry. Rejoin the road via the steps at the north end of the car park. At the top of the steps turn right and walk to the end of West Walls, turning right at the Central Plaza Hotel. Continue along, over Victoria Viaduct. To your left you can view the top of one of the twin turrets of the Citadel, built in 1541 to provide a second line of defence for the city. Here, tolls were collected for goods entering and leaving the city. The Citadel became the county's Court Houses in 1807. Go over the double pedestrian crossing on to The Nelson Bridge – erected over the River Caldew in the 1850s to connect the city with the new industrial suburb, Denton Holme.

Below and Right: Carlisle Castle.

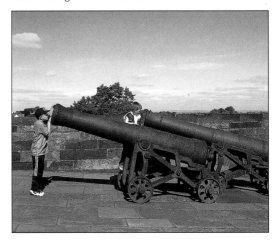

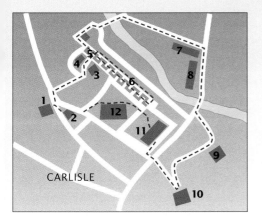

CARLISLE

Carry on over Nelson Bridge, ahead you will see **Dixon's Chimney & Shaddon Mill** 7. Dixon's Chimney was the largest of its kind in the country (originally over 300ft tall) when the factory was built in 1836. Now a listed Grade II building, Dixon's Chimney benefited from extensive, essential conservation repairs in 1998 with financial help from the Heritage Lottery Fund, English Heritage and Carlisle City Council. Note the steam engine house and boiler house (for seven boilers) between the octagonal chimney and the mill.

Just beyond the Chimney and Mill Gallery on the right hand side you will see **Linton Visitor Centre** 8. Linton Weaving Mill was founded in 1912 by Scotsman William Linton, whose great friend and Paris couturier Captain Molyneux introduced him to the Paris couture houses and, in particular, Coco Chanel. Continue along, heading for Castle Way. Look to your left and see the original building of Carrs Biscuit Works – now McVities. Cross Castle Way using the double pedestrian crossing. Ahead of you is the site of the former **Old Brewery** 9. The brewery was state owned because the Home Office took over all the public houses in Carlisle in 1916, closing a vast number in the process – the reason given was for a high level of drunkenness amongst the munitions workers at the armaments factory at nearby Gretna.

Once you have crossed Castle Way, carry on straight ahead and you can see the imposing sight of the great medieval fortress that is **Carlisle Castle** 10. It was first built after William II relieved Carlisle of two centuries of Scottish domination in 1092. Since then, it has often been the scene of turbulent conflict between the two nations, being fought over fairly consistently until the union of the crowns in 1603. It then fell into Scottish hands again during the Civil War and the Jacobite Rising 100 years later. **Tullie House Museum & Art Gallery** 11 was originally a Jacobean building (built in 1689, it is the oldest domestic building in Carlisle). Now it is an award-winning museum, offering a wealth of interactive displays encouraging you to journey back in time. Leave Tullie House by the rear exit and enjoy a walk through the grounds and through the wrought iron gates on to Abbey Street. Turn left here and enter the peaceful **Cathedral precinct** 12 through Prior Slee's gateway (dating from 1572). The Cathedral was founded in 1122 with stained glass windows from the 14th-20th centuries.

OPENING TIMES

Carlisle Castle (English Heritage), open daily 9.30am-6pm (April-Sept), 10am-5pm (Oct), 10am-4pm (Nov-March). Closed 24-26 Dec & 1 Jan. **01228 591922**. Admission charge.

Guildhall, open 1pm-4pm Thurs-Sun (Good Friday-Sept) **01228 534781**.

St Cuthbert's Church and Tithe Barn, for information **01228 532515**.

Linton Visitor Centre, open all year 9.30am-5pm Mon-Sat. Ring for details of exhibition opening hours. **01228 527569**. Free admission.

Tullie House Museum & Art Gallery, open all year 10am-5pm Mon-Sat, noon-5pm Sun. **01228 534781**. Admission charge.

Furness Abbey.

Wood, glass and stone –
THE FURNESS PENINSULA

Length: About 15 miles, one/two days

Starting point: Stott Park Bobbin Mill, Cumbria

This picturesque part of England is full of the most interesting buildings – from the soaring ruins of Furness Abbey to one of the best preserved mills in the country.

Set amongst magnificent scenery on the west side of Lake Windermere **Stott Park Bobbin Mill** ① is now a preserved industrial monument. The mill was built in 1835 and was worked continuously until 1971. It is scarcely different in appearance today than it was over 100 years ago and is now a working museum where you can witness the whole process of bobbin making. The mill also features a working static steam engine. It is

a rare survivor of mills that were once common in the Lake District. Travel south on the A592, join the A590 at Newby Bridge until you reach **Haverthwaite** ②. In the hamlet of Low Wood, Haverthwaite, you can visit Artcrystal – a hand-engraving crystal studio and watch a demonstration of the unique and rare skill of hand-engraving in the old, listed Gunpowder Works. At Abbots Reading Farm, $^1/_2$m from Haverthwaite crossroads, you can visit the working Lakeland Farm and Museum. The farm is gradually reverting to farming native and rare breeds of livestock, which can be seen in the enclosures. There is also an extensive collection of vintage agricultural machinery to give an insight into the farming methods of times gone by.

Continue on the A590 to **Ulverston** ③. This delightful town with its unique charm, fascinating ginnels and cobbled streets boasts an array of claims to fame. Ulverston was granted its market charter in 1280 and the colourful Street Market continues to be held every Thursday and Saturday when the world champion Town Crier welcomes visitors.

The world's only Laurel and Hardy Museum has a small 1920's-style cinema showing their classic films and there is also a wealth of memorabilia to be seen.

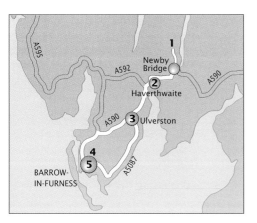

Stott Park Bobbin Mill (English Heritage), open daily 10am-6pm (April-Sept), 10am-5pm (Oct). Closed Nov-March. **01539 531087**. Admission charge.

Artcrystal, Haverthwaite, open daily 10am-4pm (mid Jan-Christmas). **01539 531796**.

Lakeland Farm and Museum, open 10.30am-5pm Sun, Mon, Tues (May-mid Sept). **01539 531203**.

Furness Abbey (English Heritage), open daily 10am-6pm (April-Sept), 10am-5pm (Oct). 10am-1pm, 2-4pm (Nov-March). Closed 24-26 Dec and 1 Jan. **01946 63222**. Admission charge.

Dock Museum, open 10am-5pm Wed-Fri, 11am-5pm Sat-Sun (Oct), 10.30am-4pm Wed-Fri, 12-4pm Sat-Sun (Nov-Easter). **01229 894444**.

Cumbria Crystal, based in Ulverston, is one of the last firms in the UK making crystal exclusively by hand and visitors are welcome to watch the blowers and to buy the finished products. At the nearby Heron Glass Visitor Centre, you can watch glass makers transform molten glass, Venetian style, into a unique range of art glass.

Head towards Barrow-in-Furness on the A590 and you will see signposts for **Furness Abbey** ④. The abbey, with its stunning red sandstone structures, was founded in 1127. At the time of the suppression, this was the second wealthiest Cistercian abbey in England. Its wealth had stemmed from its extensive lands and iron deposits. Although many of the buildings have gone, parts of the church stand almost to their full height, while in the east range of the cloister there survives an ornate chapter house and a fine series of arches.

Rejoin the A590 and travel into **Barrow-in-Furness** ⑤. The modern history of Barrow began in 1846 with the birth of the Furness Railway, built to transport local iron ore and slate out of the area. A visit to the Dock Museum will explain the proud history of the town's industrial heritage, which includes leading the world in ship and submarine building. The museum is suspended in a Victorian Graving Dock.

Stott Park Bobbin Mill.

John Craven

As a young Yorkshire lad I was convinced nowhere on earth could hold a candle to the Dales, but then I moved to the North East and discovered that between the Tees and the Tweed lies a landscape to match. My beloved Dales lead seamlessly to the Durham moors – the territory of the Prince Bishops, with thriving market towns such as Barnard Castle (I was at the sheep sales there not long ago). The upland scenery is magnificent, yet all around are reminders that this area – the first to see railway trains – was in at the start of the industrial revolution.

Then across **Hadrian's Wall** to the glorious wilds of Northumberland. Over the years, I've been amazed how many people "down south" simply have no idea what lies between Newcastle upon Tyne and the Scottish border – and what a gem they are missing. From Roman remains to ruined medieval castles, there is history galore; its coastline – with the **Farne Islands** and **Holy Island** – is my favourite anywhere in the UK, and it's hard to beat the beauty of the **River Coquet**.

Many winters ago, I was walking along its banks near Warkworth when I spotted my first deer. Startled by our presence, it swam across, scampered up the far bank and ran into the woods, leaving its footprints in the snow. It was a sight I will never forget.

Right: Dunstanburgh Castle.

From **the strong** came forth **SWEETNESS**

Length: About 6 miles one/two days

Starting point: Berwick-upon-Tweed, Northumberland

Near the border town of Berwick-upon-Tweed, powerful castles were established to protect land and people in time of conflict between England and Scotland. Today, you can ride on a model railway, visit a cornmill powered by a waterwheel, hear the story of border warfare and the Battle of Flodden in an award-winning exhibition at Etal Castle, admire a unique scheme of 19th-century wall paintings with villagers used as models and tour the once mighty fortress of Norham Castle.

Start at **Berwick-upon-Tweed** ❶ where, adjacent to the railway station and west of the town centre, there are the remains of a 12th-century castle. The Ramparts are remarkably complete 16th-century town fortifications with gateways and projecting bastions. The Barracks are amongst the earliest purpose-built barracks and have changed little since 1717. An exhibition 'By Beat of Drum' recreates scenes from the life of British infantrymen. The Main Guard, a Georgian guard house, is near the quay. From Berwick-upon-Tweed, take the A698 towards Coldstream.

One mile after the A1 roundabout, turn right to **Horncliffe** ❷. The Chain Bridge Honey Farm is signposted. The farm has an exhibition and observation hives. The Chain Bridge (short walk) was constructed in 1820 and was the first suspension bridge to carry commercial traffic. From Horncliffe, drive back towards the A698, but turn right on to the B6470 to Norham before you get to the main road.

Norham Castle ❸, one of the border strongholds, was built in the 12th century by the then Bishop of Durham. This massive castle withstood repeated attacks in the 13th and 14th centuries and was thought to be impregnable. But in 1513, it was stormed by the forces of James IV of Scotland and partially destroyed. From Norham, return to the A698 and follow the road south to turn left to the village of **Etal** ❹. The 14th-century border castle houses a major award-winning exhibition about the castle, border warfare and the Battle of Flodden, which took place nearby in 1513.

From Etal, follow the B6354 south and take a left turn to **Letham Hill,** ❺ where a working smithy can be found. The smithy specialises in wrought iron work and commissions large or small are undertaken. In the nearby woodwork shop, examples of handmade furniture, wood turning and spinning wheels made from locally grown hardwoods can be found. Follow the B6354 south turning right to **Heatherslaw** ❻, where you will find a beautifully-restored, 19th-century water-powered corn mill. The huge wooden water wheel is used to grind locally-grown wheat into wholemeal flour, which is used by local bakers. A 15" gauge steam railway runs from Heatherslaw to Etal village. The return journey of almost four miles takes 40 minutes.

From Heatherslaw follow the B6354, bearing left onto the B6353 to **Ford** village ❼. The castle dates back to the 14th century. Prior to the Battle of Flodden in 1513, James IV of Scotland stayed here. The castle is now a

Above: Etal Castle.
Right: Norham Castle.
Left Below: Berwick Barracks.

residential and outdoor study centre. Lady Waterford Hall – now the Village Hall – is notable for the large water colour murals that decorate the walls. The murals, which have just undergone major conservation work, depict children of the village and their families as characters from well-known Bible stories.

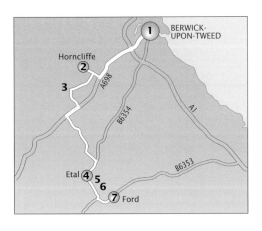

OPENING TIMES

Berwick Barracks (English Heritage), open daily 10am-6pm (April-Nov), 10am-5pm (Oct), 10am-1pm, 2pm-4pm Wed-Sun (Nov-March). Closed 24-26 Dec and 1 Jan. **01289 304493**. Admission charge.

Chain Bridge Honey Farm, open 10.30am-5pm Mon-Sat, 2pm-5pm Sun (April-Oct), 9am-5pm Mon-Fri (Nov-March) **01289 386362**. Free entry.

Norham Castle (English Heritage), open daily 10am-6pm (April-Nov), 10am-5pm (Oct). Closed Nov-March. **01289 382329**. Admission charge.

Etal Castle (English Heritage), open daily 10am-6pm (April-Nov), 10am-5pm (Oct). Closed Nov-March. **01890 820332**. Admission charge.

Letham Hill Workshops, open 10am-5pm all year. **01890 820317**.

Heatherslaw Corn Mill, open daily 10am-6pm (April-Sept), 10am-5pm (Oct). **01890 820338**. Admission charge. Trains daily (March-Oct), ticket office and shop 9.45am-4.30pm.

Ford Castle, open for guided tours by appointment. **01890 820257**.

Lady Waterford Hall, open daily 10.30am-12.30pm, 1.30pm-5.30pm (April-Oct). **01890 820338**. Admission charge.

Left: Dunstanburgh Castle.

The **Northumberland** ## **COASTAL ROUTE**

Length: About 35 miles, one day

Starting point: Belford, Northumberland

An exciting trail including houses, castles and parks that border this spectacular coastline.

From Belford on the A1 take the B1342 to the impressive coastal fortress of **Bamburgh Castle** ❶. Bamburgh was the birthplace of national heroine Grace Darling. Her body lies in the village churchyard opposite a museum dedicated to her bravery in rescuing nine survivors from the wreck of the steamship *Forfarshire* in 1838. Follow the B1340 south from Bamburgh to **Seahouses** ❷ where boat trips are available to the Farne Islands bird and seal Sanctuaries. South of Seahouses, the small village of **Beadnell** ❸ is remarkable for its well preserved 18th-century lime kilns and delightful little

harbour. **Lower Newton by the Sea** ❹ nestles behind a superb rocky natural harbour. The quaint green is surrounded on three sides by white-washed fishermen's cottages.

The mile stretch of sands at **Embleton Bay** ❺ ends in rocks and boulders that sit at the foot of sheer basalt sea cliffs which rise dramatically out of the sea. At the top of these cliffs are the brooding and stark ruins of the largest of the Northumbrian Castles – **Dunstanburgh** ❻. The castle was built by the Earl of Lancaster in the 14th century. Dunstanburgh's remote cliff-top location saw much conflict as a Lancastrian stronghold during the 15th-century Wars of the Roses. After two sieges, Dunstanburgh finally fell to the Yorkists in 1464. The ruins, situated on a 30m high basalt crag are reached by an easy $1^1/_2$ mile coastal walk from Craster or Embleton and are noted for seabirds, wildlife and flowers. Bear right at Embleton from the B1339.

The harbour at **Craster**, ❼ built in 1906 by the local Craster family, is used by inshore coble fishermen. Craster's smokehouses still produce kippers traditionally smoked over oak wood chippings, using imported Scottish herring. Follow the road from Craster towards Alnmouth and B1339 to **Howick Hall and**

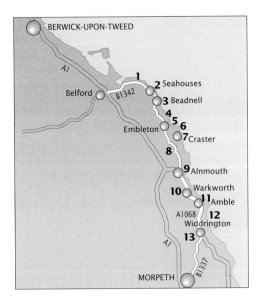

Gardens **8**, once the home of Earl Charles Grey, instigator of the 1832 Reform Act and Prime Minister of the Whig government that abolished slavery in 1833. There are extensive gardens, including a natural woodland garden in addition to the formal gardens surrounding the hall. A path leads down the bank of an idyllic little burn and along the coast to the tiny natural harbour of Howick Haven with its small beach.

Follow B1339 south to **Alnmouth** **9** – a quiet seaside village set on a high grassy bank above the mouth of the River Aln. During the mid 19th century, little coasters loaded coal, grain and fertiliser to trade around the coasts of Britain and across the North Sea. By the end of the 19th century, the port was in decline as the harbour silted up. Today the river cuts its way through hard sand beaches and walkers can travel over miles of perfect beach to the mouth of the River Coquet at Warkworth Harbour.

Follow the route 7¹/₂ miles south from Alnmouth on A1068. **Warkworth Castle** **10** has a magnificent eight-towered keep and stands on a hill above the River Coquet dominating all around it. It is an outstanding example of an aristocratic fortified residence – the favourite residence of the Percys, one of England's most powerful medieval dynasties who at times wielded more power in the north than the king himself. A little way upstream from the castle is a tiny hermitage carved into the cliff beside the River Coquet. The hermitage can be reached by rowing boat from the riverside.

Follow the A1068 from Warkworth to **Amble** **11**. Amble is situated on the south bank of the Coquet estuary, which was a harbour from Anglo-Saxon times until the mid 19th century when Amble expanded as a coal port. Four miles south of Amble on the A1068, **Druridge Bay** **12** consists of six miles of curving, golden uninterrupted beach backed by steeply-rising, flower-filled sand dunes. The open cast mines that once existed behind the sand dunes have been worked out and refilled. Follow A1068 south towards Widdrington to **Chibburn Preceptory** **13**. The ruin of the

Preceptory of St John of Jerusalem (Knights Hospitallers) dates from 1313. The attached dower house ranges round a small court and probably dates from the 1550s. There are established rights of way from the A1068 and also a route-marked path from the dunes at Druridge Bay.

OPENING TIMES

Bamburgh Castle, open daily 11am-5pm (April to Oct). **01668 214515**. Admission charge.

Grace Darling Museum, open daily (Easter-Sept). **01668 214465**. Admission charge.

Dunstanburgh Castle (English Heritage), open daily 10am-6pm (April-Sept), 10am-5pm (Oct), 10am-4pm Wed-Sun (Nov-March). Closed 24-26 Dec and I Jan. **01665 576231**. Admission charge.

Howick Hall & Gardens, open 1pm-6pm (Easter-Oct). Admission charge.

Warkworth Castle (English Heritage), open daily 10am-6pm (April-Sept), 10am-5pm (Oct), 10am-4pm (Nov-March). Closed 24-26 Dec & I Jan. **01665 711423**.

Hermitage 11am-5pm Wed, Sun & Bank Holidays (April-Sept). **01665 711423**. Admission charge.

The land of the
PRINCE BISHOPS

Length: About 35 miles, one/two days

**Starting point: Barnard Castle,
County Durham**

Norman strongholds, Roman churches and museums in the spectacular countryside of Northumbria – a land ruled for 800 years by the Prince Bishops of Durham.

Barnard Castle.

Barnard Castle ① **is an imposing** Norman stronghold at the place of a Roman river crossing point. In Barnard Castle itself, the Josephine and John Bowes Museum is a French style chateau housing art collections of national importance. The museum, just over $^1/_4$ mile east of the Market Place, was opened in 1892. $1^1/_2$ miles south east of Barnard Castle are the ruins of 12th-century **Egglestone Abbey** ②, built for the Premonstratensian order. Nearby is a fine example of a medieval pack horse bridge.

Carry on to **Rokeby Park** ③, a Palladian-style country house which was the setting for Sir Walter Scott's ballad *Rokeby*. You can see collections of 18th-century needlework paintings and furniture. Go to the A67, either via Barnard Castle or across country via Whorlton. Just south of the A67 is the picturesque village of **Piercebridge** ④, built within a Roman fort. Visible Roman remains include the East Gate and defences, courtyard building and part of the bridge that carried the Roman road, Dere Street, across the River Tees.

About $^1/_2$ mile south east of Shildon town centre is the **Timothy Hackworth Victorian and Railway Museum** ⑤. Timothy Hackworth, Superintendent of the Stockton & Darlington Railway, set up his engine works here. The works and his house are now a museum. Take the A6072 to **Bishop Auckland** ⑥, a market town which grew around the bishops' favourite country residence. At the east end of the Market Place is the castle, with its 800 acre park, now the official residence of present day bishops. The Deer House is a charming building erected in 1760 in the park for deer to shelter and find food. Take the A688 south west out of Bishop Auckland and you will find **Raby Castle** ⑦, one of the grandest castles in England. It was a stronghold of the Nevills for 400 years. Enlarged and beautified over the centuries, the medieval heart remains. The A688 will take you back to Barnard Castle.

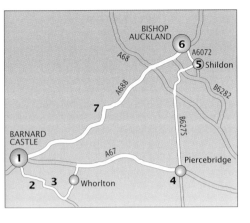

OPENING TIMES

Barnard Castle (English Heritage), open daily 10am-6pm (April-Sept), 10am-5pm (Oct), 10am-4pm Wed-Sun (Nov-March). Closed 1pm-2pm and 24-26 Dec and 1 Jan. **01833 638212**. Admission charge.

The Josephine and John Bowes Museum, open daily all year. For information **01833 690606**. Admission charge.

Egglestone Abbey (English Heritage), open at any reasonable time. Free entry.

Rokeby Park, open Mon-Tues (Spring Bank Holiday-Sept). For information **01833 637334**. Admission charge.

Piercebridge Roman Fort, open at any reasonable time. For information **01325 463795**.

Timothy Hackworth Museum, open 10am-5pm Wed-Sun (Easter-Oct). For information **01388 777999**. Admission charge.

Auckland Castle and Deer House, for park opening times **01388 601627**. Admission charge.

Raby Castle, for opening times **01833 660202**. Admission charge.

Egglestone Abbey.

Prudhoe Castle.

Begin at **Prudhoe Castle** ❶, situated 14 miles west of Newcastle via the A695 in Prudhoe. Here are the extensive remains of a 12th-century castle, set on a wooded hillside by the River Tyne. From Prudhoe Castle, turn left up the steep hill to the traffic lights in Prudhoe, and turn right on to the A695, heading west towards Corbridge and Hexham. After $4^1/_2$ miles, take the third exit (A68 north) at the roundabout. After one mile, at the next large roundabout, take the second exit (A69 towards Corbridge and Hexham).

After three miles, take the left filter and head towards **Corbridge** ❷. Corbridge Roman Site is signposted to the right, at a right-hand bend just before you get to the centre of the village. This Roman site was an early fort and supply base for Hadrian's Wall. It was occupied for longer than any other place associated with Hadrian's Wall and developed into a prosperous garrison town. The museum displays fascinating finds and remarkable sculptures. In the

Tyne **valley**
TOUR

Length: About 16 miles, one/two days

Starting point: Prudhoe Castle, Northumberland

From Prudhoe Castle, travel back in time to the Roman town at Corbridge and end your trail in historic Hexham with an exhibition about medieval outlaws.

relatively modern village of Corbridge look out for St. Andrew's Church (Saxon) and the ancient pele tower.

Aydon Castle ③ is two miles north of Corbridge. Take the A68 or the B6321 and follow the signs to Aydon Castle. It is one of the finest examples of a 13th-century manor house, built during a time of unusual peace in the Borders and then quickly fortified. From Aydon Castle, turn left out of the car park and follow a very narrow lane to join the A68. Turn left on to the A68 (south), then take the A69 to **Hexham** ④, almost three miles. In Hexham, park in the main Wentworth car park and walk up into Hexham. Look out for Hexham Gaol, now containing a lively exhibition about Border Reivers. Hexham Abbey stands next to the Market Place. The crypt is the best example from the Anglo-Saxon period and dates from 674, when the abbey was founded. In the chancel stands St. Wilfrid's Chair, where the Kings of Northumbria were crowned.

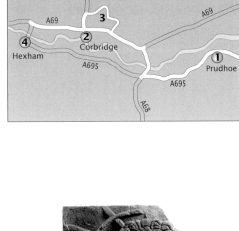

The God Apollo, Corbridge.

Aydon Castle.

OPENING
TIMES

Prudhoe Castle (English Heritage), open daily 10am-6pm (April-Sept), 10am-5pm (Oct). Closed Nov-March. **01661 833459**. Admission charge.

Corbridge Roman Site (English Heritage), open daily 10am-6pm (April-Nov), 10am-4pm Wed-Sun (Nov-March). Closed 24-26 Dec and 1 Jan. **01434 632349**. Admission charge.

Aydon Castle (English Heritage), open daily 10am-6pm (April-Sept), 10am-5pm (Oct). Closed Nov-March. **01434 632450**. Admission charge.

Above and right: Views of Warkworth Castle.

Warkworth heritage **WALK**

Length: Around 1-2 miles depending on route chosen, 2/3 hours. The walk is mainly flat, but has a short steep climb from the river bank to the castle. There is a flight of steps at the south east point of the castle.

Starting point: Warkworth Market Place

Visit Warkworth Castle, the Old Bridge and other sites for a journey through Northumbrian history. The River Coquet forms a splendid backdrop, as do the views over the coast.

From the Market Place ① by the Market Cross, (with your back to the castle), take the right hand fork (Bridge Street) for about $1/_2$ mile to the tower on the pedestrian bridge over the River Coquet. **The Old Bridge** ② is a 14th-century fortified bridge and unique in Northumberland. It is a grade II listed building. At the bridge turn left, a wooden public footpath signpost directs you to Mill Walk.

Follow the River Coquet upstream. Pass the church of **St Lawrence** ③ on your left and continue along the river bank upstream using the roadside grass verge. The church has a vaulted chancel inspired by Durham Cathedral. The road ends by a public footpath sign to Mill Walk and Howlett Hall, $3/_4$ mile. Continue along the river bank. Here you will find a public footpath signpost to **Warkworth Castle** ④, $1/_4$ mile. The first stone castle was built in 1139 when Henry, son of David I of Scotland, became Earl of Northumberland.

For the shorter walk, take the left path up hill. After a short climb, with superb views of the river, Warkworth Castle will be in front of you. At the top of the hill you

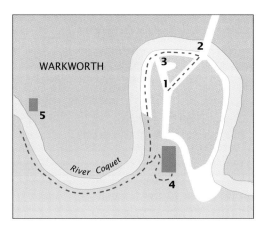

can return to the market place by going straight ahead through a gap in the wall on to Castle Street or you can continue around the castle.

For the longer walk, continue along the river bank path upstream, approximately $^1/_4$ mile to the **Hermitage** ⑤ across the river. The Hermitage was carved out of the rock in 1330-40. The chapel has many carvings. To return, retrace your steps to the public footpath signpost and take the right hand path up the hill to the castle. At the top of the hill bear right and at the top of the steps skirt left to the south of the castle and the roadside gateway. Cross the road carefully and bear left. The pavement leads on to Castle Terrace then back into the village and market place.

OPENING
TIMES

Warkworth Castle and Hermitage (English Heritage), open daily 10am-6pm (April-Sept), 10am-5pm (Oct), 10am-1pm, 2pm-4pm (Nov-March). Closed 24-26 Dec and 1 Jan. Hermitage is accessible by a rowing boat operated by English Heritage. For information **01665 711423**. Admission charge.

Janet Street-Porter

I've walked in Yorkshire for 20 years now, from the Dales to the North York Moors, becoming an expert on unpredictable weather in the process. As a general rule it is best to anticipate three major climatic changes per Yorkshire day – rain, sun, hail or wind, thunderstorm, sunny evening. I can guarantee you'll have completely different weather (involving a change of clothing) by 4pm. I'm always an optimist – if it's rainy, I start later and generally end up with a pleasantly balmy evening. I've also eaten a lot of picnics sheltering behind dry-stone walls as a gale rages, only to find if I hadn't been so greedy a sunny period was only 30 minutes away.

The best thing about walking in Yorkshire is the contrast between huge open moorland and lush valleys. **Wharfedale,** with its beautiful pattern of dry-stone walls alongside the valley floor, has limestone crags and open grassland on the tops of the fells that feel like prairie. I even love walking in the bog over **Buckden Pike.** On the North York Moors, I've followed disused railway lines for miles, dropped down into **Rievaulx** and visited Osmotherley for tea and the nicest public ladies' loo in Britain. **Whitby** is another favourite – the climb up to the Abbey and the views from the cliffs are completely exhilarating. The best walks include history and scenery; Fountains Abbey, Richmond Castle, Easby and Middleham. Yorkshire is the best county by far to fulfil that dream combination.

Right: Mount Grace Priory in autumn.

Captain Cook –
ROOTS TO ROUTES

Length: About 32 miles, one/two days

Starting point: Marton, near Middlesbrough

This trail will take you on a journey of discovery as it follows the life of Britain's most famous seafarer and explorer.

Whitby.

Captain Cook Birthplace Museum ❶ is situated in Stewart Park, Marton, near Middlesbrough, and has exciting new displays about Cook's voyages. From Stewart Park car park, turn left on to the B1380, then left on to the A172 towards Stokesley (south) to **Marton** ❷. A short distance on the right-hand side is the church where the infant Cook was baptised in 1728. Look for the memorial window to him. From Marton, continue south on the A172. After three miles turn left on to the B1292 to **Great Ayton** ❸.

Cook's family moved here when he was eight years old and he attended the village school. This is now a small museum about Cook and life in Great Ayton in the 18th century. From Great Ayton, take the A173 (north), joining the A171 to Guisborough. Take the A173 to Skelton and Brotton, then take the A174 to the picturesque fishing village of **Staithes** ❹, (12 miles from Guisborough). Cook came here aged 16 to work in William Sanderson's general stores. This has long since slipped into the sea which lashes this unstable coastline. You can visit Staithes Heritage Centre, which includes a street scene and Sanderson's shop from 1745.

From Staithes, return to the A174 and then turn left to Whitby (about nine miles).

On the way, visit St Hilda's Well in the churchyard at **Hinderwell** ❺. Cook probably worshipped at the church here, as William Sanderson, his employer, was church warden. In **Whitby** ❻, there are many sites associated with Captain Cook, and his statue dominates the West Cliff. In 1746, he was apprenticed to John and Henry Walker, whose coal ships traded up and down the east coast.

John Walker's house, where Cook lodged, in the east side of Whitby in Grape Lane. It has been carefully restored and is now the Captain Cook Memorial Museum. Rooms are furnished in mid 18th-century style with models, letters and watercolours

OPENING
TIMES

Captain Cook Birthplace Museum, open 10am-
5.30pm Tues-Sun (Summer), 9am-4pm (Winter).
01642 311211. Admission charge.

Great Ayton Museum, open daily 2pm-4.30pm
(April-Oct), 10.30am-12.30pm Mon-Sat (Aug).
01642 723911. Admission charge.

Staithes Heritage Centre, open daily 10am-5pm
(March-Dec), weekends only (Jan-Feb).
01947 841454. Admission charge.

Captain Cook Memorial Museum, open daily
9.45am-5pm (April-Oct), 11am-3pm weekends
only (March). **01947 601900**. Admission charge.

Whitby Abbey (English Heritage),open daily
10am-6pm (April-Sept), 10am-5pm (Oct),
10am-4pm (Nov-March). Closed 24-26 Dec and 1
Jan. **01947 603568**. Admission charge.

by artists who travelled with Cook on his voyages. For more information about Cook, visit Whitby Museum in Pannett Park – and for a glorious view of the mighty sea, walk up the 199 steps to Whitby Abbey. The abbey, founded by St Hilda in 657, stands on the headland where successive abbey buildings have always been a landmark for sailors. On the way, go into St Mary's Church for a fascinating glimpse of an 18th-century church interior, full of box pews. Look out for the chandelier hanging on a chain with a decorative anchor.

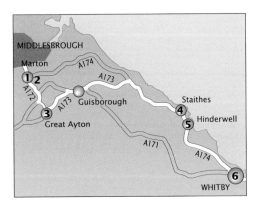

Helmsley – monks, moors and MARKETS

Length: About 8 miles, one/two days

Starting point: Byland Abbey, North Yorkshire

Whether it be the medieval floor tiles of Byland Abbey, the gardens, terraces and temples of Duncombe Park, or the Elizabethan buildings in the castle, there are historical treasures to be discovered in and around the market town of Helmsley.

Two miles south of the A170 near to Coxwold village, **Byland Abbey** ❶ is a hauntingly lovely ruin set in peaceful meadows in the shadow of the Hambleton Hills. The monastery was founded in 1134 by monks sent from Furness in Cumbria. Byland's west front is magnificent, if in ruins. Practically the whole church was paved with green and yellow glazed tiles in geometric patterns.

From Byland, take the A170 to Helmsley and visit the spectacular **Helmsley Castle** ❷. Huge earthworks, now softened to green valleys, are all that remain of the earliest castle, built by Walter Espec in the early 12th century. The oldest stonework is late 12th century, but throughout the middle ages the castle was strengthened and modernised. Although strongly defended, the castle saw no action until the Civil War of the 17th century, when after a siege by parliamentary forces, its defences were dismantled. From Helmsley Castle, re-enter the town and proceed to **Duncombe Park** ❸ whose

Top: Byland Abbey.
Above: Helmsley Castle.
Right: Rievaulx Abbey.

entrance is situated just off the market place. The house was built in the 18th century for Thomas Duncombe, who had previously resided in the Elizabethan buildings at Helmsley Castle. The main showrooms are a fine example of the type of grand interior popular at the turn of the century. The early 18th-century green garden takes up 35 acres in nearly 300 acres of dramatic parkland.

The walled garden (entrance near the main Helmsley car park) was built in the grounds of Duncombe Park in 1780 to supply the house with fruit, vegetables and flowers. Years later, it became a commercial market garden, but it returned to nature when the business ceased in 1980. In 1994, a project was launched to return the garden to its original layout and now it is possible to visit and see the progress that is being made. Ideally situated in a hollow between the earthworks on which Helmsley Castle stands and the gentle slopes of Duncombe Park, the garden is flourishing.

From Helmsley, follow the B1257 west for approximately two miles and take the minor road to **Rievaulx Abbey** 4 . There you can explore the extensive remains of the largest monastic establishment in Britain. From modest beginnings in 1132 sprang one of the wealthiest monasteries of medieval England and the first Cistercian monastery in the North. The abbey was suppressed in 1538, but the story of Rievaulx can still be read in the magnificent Gothic architecture of its ruined buildings, which retain a record of the drastic changes that happened in monastic life during its 400 year history.

The Terrace, situated above Rievaulx Abbey, was built in 1758 by Thomas Duncombe (of Duncombe Park) for elaborate family picnics. There are two mid-18th-century temples, of which the Ionic temple has elaborate ceiling paintings and fine 18th-century furniture, whilst the basement contains a permanent exhibition on English landscape design in the 18th-century.

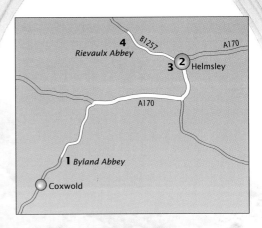

OPENING
TIMES

Byland Abbey (English Heritage), open daily 10am-6pm (April-Sept), 10am-5pm (Oct). Closed 1pm-2pm and Nov-March. **01347 868614**. Admission charge.

Helmsley Castle (English Heritage), open daily 10am-6pm (April-Sept), 10am-5pm (Oct), 10am-4pm Wed-Sun (Nov-March). Closed 1pm-2pm and 24-26 Dec and 1 Jan. **01439 770442**. Admission charge.

Duncombe Park, open 11am-6pm Sun-Thurs (April-Oct) and Sun-Fri (May-Sept). **01439 770213**. Admission charge.

Helmsley Walled Garden, open 10.30am-5pm Fri-Sun (April-Oct), 12 noon-4pm (Nov-March). **01439 771427**. Admission charge.

Rievaulx Abbey (English Heritage), open daily 10am-6pm (April-June & Sept), 9.30am-7pm (July-Aug), 10am-5pm (Oct), 10am-4pm (Nov-March). Closed 24-26 Dec and 1 Jan. **01439 798228**. Admission charge.

Rievaulx Terrace and Temples (National Trust), open daily 10.30-6pm (April-Oct). **01439 798340**. Admission charge.

Pickering Castle.

The **pleasures** of **PICKERING**

Length: About $^1/_2$ mile, two/three hours

Starting point: The Market Place, Pickering

Explore the many historic buildings in this pretty Yorkshire town and visit a splendid motte and bailey castle with spectacular views over the surrounding countryside.

Starting at the bottom, where the Market Place ❶ joins Bridge Street, go up the left side of the main street (looking across to the stalls on Monday market day). Pass the Bay Horse Inn, a hostelry for Cromwellian troops in the 17th century. Next is the White Swan, a former farmer's inn from which the 'England Rejoice' stagecoach once ran across the moors to Whitby. At the corner shop, turn into Burgate and walk up it towards

Pickering Castle. **Burgate** ❷ was the 'borough' founded in King John's time on land between the settlement and the Norman castle. At the junction of Burgate with **Castlegate** ❸, look left down Brant Hill, which descends steeply to Park Street. Here, the old Whitby road branches off to the right.

Further along Castlegate, on the left behind an old white cottage with a stone horse-mounting block, is a Friend's Meeting House of 1793. Go through the side gate to see the quiet burial ground of Priestmans and Rowntrees, two well-known local Quaker families. From here, there is a fine view of the valley. **Pickering Castle** ❹ is entered over a dry moat. Inside you will find a splendid motte and bailey castle with much of the original walls, towers and keep preserved. You can still climb to the crest of the motte to gain a fine view of the countryside around. On leaving the castle, walk down the left side of Castlegate. **Willowgate** ❺ is reached via the second left turn out of Castlegate. John Wesley first preached here at No 9 Willowgate. Further down, there is a restored cruck timber and stone house, once an inn. **Pickering Church** ❻ is reached by a sharp turn left from Willowgate up the steps into the churchyard. Note how the old church alehouse was reached directly from on the north side. **Hallgarth** ❼ is found by continuing along the lower of the churchyard paths. Church Lane (as it is called) runs alongside an attractive Georgian brick-built house, a former vicarage, facing into Hallgarth.

Just above this is the Parish Hall, previously a National School, founded, 1857. At the crest of the rise is a large house, previously another and later vicarage, but now a private house. This is on the site of the original Hall, which King Henry I gave to the Deans of York when the castle replaced it. On the right hand side at the bottom is the Lumley Rest Garden, once the old cattle market. The drinking fountain and several seats commemorate John Wilson, a local Labour pioneer. **Eastgate car park** ⑧ has the Tourist Information Centre and public conveniences. **Hungate** ⑨ to the west, once a dumping ground for butcher's offal, took its name from the hounds it attracted. Walk along it to see the plaque on the large

house jutting into the road where Dr A J Kirk lived and gathered the nucleus of the collection of bygones now at the Castle Museum, York, which he founded. Many properties nearby have a wide covered access for farm wagons. Further along, there is a former Wesleyan Chapel and graveyard, now a private garden. The chapel has been converted by the Pickering Musical Society into its Kirk Theatre.

Continue over the footbridge and cross at the traffic lights to return along north side of Hungate. Further along is the 18th-century building housing the United Reform Church. Ignore the long alley called Straight Lane – which runs through to the Market Place and passes the Old Central Cinema, now an auction room – and go through the short alley, further along into **Smiddy Hill** ⑩, or Old Cattle Market, which has the Horsehoe Inn and the Lettered Board. **Birdgate** ⑪ sweeps to the left at the top of Smiddy Hill. To the right there are 17th-century houses tucked under the church wall and a fine Georgian town house (now an office) in the corner. Amongst the shops on the left, the Black Swan is prominent, a great old Georgian stage-coach inn visited by Charles Dickens. **Market Place** ① (low side) has many Georgian and Victorian buildings. Taylor's greengrocery (No 42) conceals a 15th-century house, while Paddisons (No 37) has a Victorian door complete with former pharmacy's advertisements. The Conservative Club and its neighbour were built for a whaling captain, and St George House was the George Inn. **Bridge Street** ⑫ lies across the junction at the bottom of Market Place. Just over the old bridge is Beck Isle Museum.

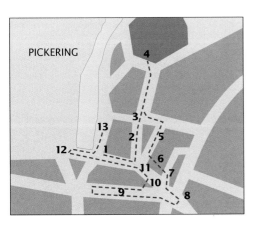

OPENING TIMES

Pickering Castle (English Heritage), open daily 10am-6pm (April-Sept), 10am-5pm (Oct), 10am-4pm Wed-Sun (Nov-March).
Closed 1pm-2pm and 24-26 Dec and 1 Jan.
0171 474989. Admission charge.

Beck Isle Museum
01751 473653. Admission charge.

Opposite is the town's Memorial Hall, once a steam-powered corn mill. Potter Hill, just beyond, has an Italianate Methodist Chapel and a Roman Catholic Church with a piece of sculptured work by Eric Gill. If you return to Ropery junction, **Park Street** ⑬ lies to the left, leading to the railway station designed by G T Andrews in 1846. Opposite is the Station Hotel where legend has it the navvies once made such a noise that they turned a prominent townsman to drink.

The real
SOUTH YORKSHIRE

Length: About 32 miles, one/two days

Starting point: Cannon Hall

Delve into a slice of country life that takes in castles and country houses, museums, parks and gardens and a landscape devised by Capability Brown.

Situated off the A635 between Barnsley and Huddersfield, **Cannon Hall** 1 has 70 acres of historic parkland. A walled garden, dating from the 1760s, can be enjoyed all year round. For 200 years the house, designed by John Carr of York, was the home of the Spencer Stanhope family. It is now a museum with fine collections of pottery, furniture and paintings.

From Cannon Hall, follow the A635 towards junction 37 of the A1(M) and three miles north of Doncaster is the Museum of South Yorkshire Life at **Cusworth Hall** 2. This imposing 18th-century country house, in part the work of James Paine, is set in an extensive landscaped park. The museum houses evocative displays of the changing home, work and social life of local communities over the past 250 years.

Situated between the A635 and the A638 you will find **Brodsworth Hall** 3, an outstanding example of a Victorian country house, which has survived almost completely intact since the 1860s with most of its original contents. The garden incorporates both formal and informal features, all contained within magnificent parkland. From Brodsworth, return to the A1(M) south and at junction 36 take the

A630 to **Conisbrough** 4. The stone castle was built in about 1180. The castle's fame today is mainly due to Sir Walter Scott's novel *Ivanhoe*.

From Conisbrough railway station you can take a self-propelled bike train from the car park and pedal to the entrance of the **Earth Centre** 5. Here is a world where exploring the future is fun and you can discover how to put the ideas into practice.

From Conisbrough, join the B6376 to Maltby and from there take the A634 to **Roche Abbey** 6. This Cistercian monastery was founded in 1147 and is set in an enchanting valley landscaped by Capability Brown. The abbey suffered from the effects of the Black Death in the mid-14th century and by 1380 the community had been reduced to 15. In the mid-18th

Roche Abbey.

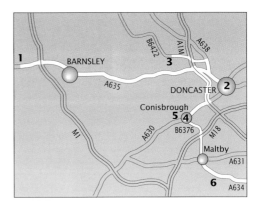

century, Capability Brown was employed to reorganise the landscape, which resulted in severe losses in the remaining fabric of the Abbey.

OPENING TIMES

Cannon Hall, open 10.30am-5pm Tues-Sat, 12noon-5pm Sun (April-Oct). **01226 790270**.

Museum of South Yorkshire Life, open weekdays 10am-5pm, 11am-5pm Sat, 1pm-5pm Sun. **01302 782342**. Free entry.

Brodsworth Hall (English Heritage), open 1pm-6pm Tues-Sun (April-Oct), 11am-4pm (Nov-March). **01302 722598**. Admission charge.

Conisbrough Castle (English Heritage), open daily 10am-5pm April-Sept), 10am-4pm (Oct-March). Closed 24-26 Dec and 1 Jan. shop. Castle managed by the Ivanhoe Trust. **01709 863329**. Admission charge.

The Earth Centre. **01709 512000** for opening times.

Roche Abbey (English Heritage), open daily 10am-6pm (April-Sept), 10am-5pm (Oct). Closed Nov-March. **01709 812739**. Admission charge.

Brodsworth hall.

Easby Abbey.

The Richmond
Drummer Boy WALK

**Length: About three miles,
one/two hours**

Starting point: Market Place

For centuries, Richmond has been the centre of military activity. At the end of the 18th century, the town was often garrisoned by Militia – companies of 70-100 foot soldiers with two or three drummer boys, often aged no more than eight to 15.

Just off the Market Place is **Richmond Castle 1** built around 1071 by Alan 'The Red' of Brittany. He had been rewarded with a vast amount of land in Yorkshire by William the Conqueror for his services during the invasion of England. It was not until a century later that the huge stone tower, called the Keep, was constructed under the direction of Earl Conan 'The Little'. The town of Richmond

grew to the north of the castle. In the late 18th century, the cobbled Market Place was very different from what it is today.

Holy Trinity Church, now the **Green Howards Museum 2**, was surrounded by shops and buildings. There was a three-storey Tollbooth in front of the Town Hall and the medieval cross has just been replaced by the present obelisk with a finial on top. A vast reservoir is situated under the obelisk linked by water conduits. Walk down across the cobblestones to the north east corner of the Market Place to a street leading north called **Frenchgate 3**. At the north east and lower end of the Market Place is one of the oldest parts of Richmond, which is believed to have been occupied by the Normans who built the castle. It is called Frenchgate, formerly 'Frankesgate'. The old cobblestone street leads down a dip past Swale House and up to the Green Howards War Memorial on top of the hill.

Turn north down Frenchgate past Swale House and turn right along Station Road past Richmond Lower School. **St Mary's Church 4** dating from the 12th century, is across the road on your left. However, by the mid 19th century the structure deteriorated and it was completely refurbished between 1858-9. Walk down Station Road to the far end of the

Richmond Castle.

OPENING TIMES

Richmond Castle (English Heritage), open daily 10am-6pm (April-Sept), 10am-4pm (Nov-March). Closed 24-26 Dec and 1 Jan. **01748 822493**. Admission charge.

Green Howards Museum, open daily. Details of opening **01748 822133**. Admission charge.

Easby Abbey (English Heritage), open daily 10am-6pm (April-Nov). **0191 261 1585**. Admission charge.

churchyard and turn left down a narrow snicket called Lombards Wynd. After about 30m you will reach a right turning along a path called Easby Low Road. On your left down the path you will see a green sign indicating Easby Abbey – $^3/_4$ mile. Lombards Wynd is an ancient route from the water's edge to the north of Frenchgate. Easby Low Road is the old path to Easby Abbey along the east bank of the River Swale. It leads upwards through Easby Wood with the fast flowing river down on the right. At the end of the wood, where a track leads down to the river, there is a gateway leading into a wide field.

The Drummer Boy Stone ⑤ marks the spot where the soldiers last heard the sound of drumming. (The stone leans against the right hand gatepost.) Continue past the Drummer Boy Stone down the path that leads alongside the wire fence of the field in the direction of **Easby Abbey** ⑥. Continue south down the same path to a car park. To the left is the ancient church of **St Agatha** ⑦. Inside the church are some remarkable 13th-century frescoes. From the church, walk towards the gravel path that leads along the bank of the River Swale. After about 100 metres, you cross the old metal bridge and travel north along the **old railway track** ⑧. Richmond was once linked to the main Darlington to York railway line, discontinued in 1970. The old

railway station has been converted into a garden centre. Continue for about $^1/_2$m north along the old railway track past the former railway station, on to the A6136 road. Turn right and cross Station Bridge over the River Swale. Take the first gateway on the left which leads on to a path by the side of the river.

The grassy banks leading down to the river below the former Grammar School – now Richmond Lower School – are called the **Batts** ⑨. As you climb slowly upwards along the path, it is possible to see the water falls and weir on the River Swale below the castle walls. The footpath leads on to Park Wynd and then to Millgate, the road that leads up to the Market Place.

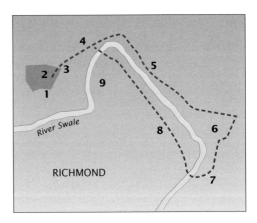

Alan Titchmarsh

"Poor you!" my friends would regularly remark during the ten years when I spent half my time in the Midlands presenting *Pebble Mill*. They looked upon it as a cultural wilderness – the inspiration for Blake's "dark satanic mills", more than likely.

But I knew they were wrong, because after the lunchtime programme had finished I would go walkabout. It was then that I discovered the riches of Birmingham's past, and its often stupendous architecture. I found stately homes and country walks within spitting distance of the city centre, and I began to realise that the Midlands offered rich pickings to anyone wanting to step back in time. I've marvelled at industrial achievements in **Ironbridge,** dreamed on the ramparts of **Kenilworth Castle** and tramped across **Wenlock Edge.**

This is a part of the country that remains close to my heart, not only because many of its beauties are unsung, but also because they are here in infinite variety. We all need to escape from time to time, and no matter where you are in this patch of Britain that links north with south and east with Wales, a little exploration will reveal a wealth of secrets.

Right: Wrought-iron steps at Witley Court.

Fire! Fire! Blasts, burns and **BANGS!**

Length: About 100 miles, one/two days

Starting point: Rushton Triangular Lodge, Northamptonshire.

Fire! A basic element taken for granted in the 20th century – but one which has left its mark in the East Midlands. Follow our 'hot' trail and discover unusual sites linked to Gun Powder Plot conspiracies, Civil War battles and slightings – and collapsing flag poles!

Above: Old John Tower, Bradgate Park.
Below: Lyddington Bede House.
Background: Ashby de la Zouch castle.

Rushton Triangular Lodge ❶ **is a most** unusual folly with connections to the Gun Powder Plot. It was built in 1597 by Thomas Tresham, whose son, Francis, ended up with his head stuck on a pole in Northampton following the conspirator's discovery. Continue along the A6003 and follow the signs to **Lyddington Bede House ❷**, next to the church, in Lyddington. This former palace of the Bishops of Lincoln, later converted to an almshouse, has a number of bedesman's rooms. Find out how the wardens kept a check on the state of the bedesman's fires!

Continue along the A6003 and turn left at the Junction with the A47 and follow this into Leicester. Follow the signs to the **Gas Museum ❸**, (Aylestone Road), where you can discover how an all-gas 1920s kitchen looked, as well as a gas-powered hairdryer and radio! Coming out of Leicester City Centre, follow the A50 and then signs for **Bradgate Country Park ❹** (near Newtown Linford). In the park is 'Old John' where a windmill once stood. The windmill was destroyed by fire. Shortly afterwards in 1786, at the coming of age celebrations of the son and heir of the fifth Earl of Stamford, an immense bonfire was built in the park. Old John, the miller, was put in charge, but the pole at the centre of the bonfire collapsed and fell on his head, causing a fatal injury. A monument was erected in his memory, shaped like a mug-of-ale.

Head south and rejoin the A50, and on to the A511 through Coalville, following signs for Ashby de la Zouch. En-route you may wish to explore **Snibston Discovery Park ❺** and experience the working conditions of a 19th-century coalface in the Extractives Gallery. **Ashby de la Zouch Castle** 6 was blown apart by gun powder in 1649 following a two year Civil War siege. You can see the damage the blast caused to Hastings Tower. Just south of Ashby is the village of **Moira** 7, where you can explore an early 19th-century blast furnace building. Follow the A511 back to the M1, and head south to Junction 21A.

Follow the signs to **Kirby Muxloe** 8 and explore the castle, which displays very unusual gunports. Head back on to the M1 and continue south to Junction 19 – follow the A14 east. After about eight miles you will reach **Naseby** 9, scene of the decisive Civil War battle of 1645, where horse, rather than musket fire, won the day for the Parliamentarians. The A14 leads back to Rushton.

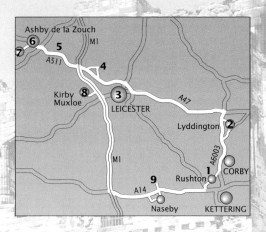

The Triangular Lodge.

OPENING TIMES

Rushton Triangular Lodge (English Heritage), open daily 10am-6pm (April-Sept), 10am-5pm (Oct). Closed Nov-March. **01536 710761**. Admission charge.

Lyddington Bede House (English Heritage), open daily 10am-6pm (April-Sept), 10am-5pm (Oct). Closed Nov-March. **01572 822438**. Admission charge.

Gas Museum, open 12.30pm-4.30pm Tues-Fri. **0116 250 3190**. Access ground floor only for disabled visitors.

Bradgate Park Folly, open 12pm-5pm Tues-Fri (April-Oct), 1pm-5pm Sat-Sun (Nov-Mar). **0116 236 2713**.

Snibston Discovery Park, Open daily. Information on **01530 510851/813256**.

Ashby de la Zouch Castle (English Heritage), open daily, 10am-6pm (April-Sept), 10am-5pm (Oct). 10am-4pm Wed-Sun (Nov-March). Closed 24-26 Dec and 1 Jan. **01530 413343**. Admission charge.

Moira Furnace. **01283 224667**.

Kirby Muxloe Castle (English Heritage), open noon-5pm Sat-Sun and bank holidays (April-Oct). **01533 386886**. Admission charge.

Above: Brodsworth Hall kitchen.
Top Right: Wingfield Manor.
Bottom Right: Hardwick Old Hall.

Let's go COOKING

Length: About 85 miles, one/two days.

Starting point: Wingfield Manor, Derbyshire

What did our ancestors eat? What were their cooking arrangements? Take our trail and peer up chimneys, into bread ovens, and cross from parlours to pantries – you'll be close enough to smell history!

On entering the remains of **Wingfield Manor** ① visitors are first greeted by the great kitchen – two wide fireplaces on either side of the door were used for roasting and heating water, while a third contained two large ovens. You can even peer up the chimney – at one stage plumes of smoke would have risen from food prepared for Mary Queen of Scots

during her imprisonment at Wingfield. Head via Alfreton and the A38 to join the M1 at junction 28, coming off at junction 29 and follow the signs for **Hardwick Old Hall** ②. This was the family home of Bess of Hardwick, one of the most famous women of the Elizabethan age. The lobby off the main hall has a service hatch leading through to the kitchen. Inside the kitchen is a great fireplace where meat was roasted on a spit. To the right of the fireplace, doors lead down into the Pastry, a room for baking, and the huge fireplace contains several deep bread ovens. The little cellar room next to it was a larder. The kitchens in the adjacent New Hall, complete with condiments, are well worth seeing. Head back to junction 29, and follow the signs for **Bolsover Castle** ③. Known to have been built in 1613, the two kitchens contain remains of hot plates, a stillage (a raised bench for storing of wine or beer casks), fireplaces and access to what were service rooms, pantries and larders. Head east along the A632, turning left on to the A60, then east on the A57, before joining the A1. Head north for a short distance before taking a right turn on to the A620 towards Gainsborough.

Gainsborough Old Hall ④ has a magnificent Great Hall and fully-equipped kitchen, displayed as it would have been in preparation for a Grand Feast. Here you can smell medieval foods and learn of the origins of some everyday culinary terms. An audio tour describes what residents of the hall would have feasted on in 1483, when Richard III stayed – including swan, game, fresh fish, fancy pastries, blancmange and marzipan. And be sure not to miss the meat room, containing such delights as wild boar, deer, pheasants and rabbits. From Gainsborough, head west along the A631, then north along the A638.

A short distance north west of Doncaster you will see signs for **Brodsworth Hall and Gardens** ⑤. Brodsworth displays Victorian life in all its eccentricities. The servants domain, the Victorian kitchen, is one of the Hall's most delightful features. Its 'Eagle Range' by Farr and Sons of Doncaster and its grained dressers still contain a vast range of cooking utensils. Blocked up after use by the army in the Second World War, the range has only recently been opened up and retains all the dirt and grime of 50 years abandonment.

Gainsborough Old Hall.
(Inner Visions)

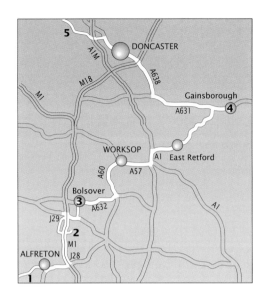

OPENING TIMES

Hardwick Old Hall (English Heritage), open 10am-6pm Wed-Sun (April-Sept), 10am-5pm Wed-Sun (Oct). Closed Nov-March. **01246 850431**. Admission charge.

Hardwick Hall (National Trust), opening times **01246 850430**. Admission charge.

Wingfield Manor (English Heritage), open 10am-6pm Wed-Sun (April-Sept), 10am-5pm Wed-Sun (Oct), 10am-1pm & 2pm-4pm Sat-Sun (Nov-March). Closed 24-26 Dec and 1 Jan. **01773 832060**. Admission charge.

Bolsover Castle (English Heritage), open daily 10am-6pm (April-Sept), 10am-5pm (Oct), 10am-4pm Wed-Sun (Nov-March). Closed 24-26 Dec and 1 Jan. **01246 823349**. Admission charge.

Gainsborough Old Hall (English Heritage), open 10am-5pm Mon-Sat (Easter Sun-Oct), 2pm-5.30pm Sun (Nov-Easter Sat). Closed Good Friday, 24-26 Dec and 1 Jan. **01427 612669**. Admission charge.

Brodsworth Hall (English Heritage), open 1pm-6pm Tues-Sun (April-Nov), 11am-4pm Sat-Sun (Nov-March). **01302 722598**.

Of **kings** and queens
& CROSSES TO BEAR...

Length: About 106 miles, one/two days

Starting point: Geddington, Northamptonshire

Explore a quiet area of Northamptonshire, 'The Rose of the Shires', and discover its royal connections, Civil War intrigues and religious persecution. The trail links Northamptonshire's two Eleanor Crosses, at Geddington and Hardingstone.

Geddington's Eleanor Cross **1** is a wonderfully preserved cross recalling the devotion of Edward I to his wife Eleanor of Castile – she bore him 13 children! A series of 12 Eleanor Crosses were constructed between 1291 and 1294, marking the resting places of her funeral cortege from Harby in Nottinghamshire to Westminster Abbey. Follow the A427 to Oundle, taking a small side trip south at Lower Benefield (approx three miles down

Kirby Hall.

minor roads), following the signs for **Lyveden New Bield** **2**. (The property requires approximately $^1/_2$ mile walk from the parking area). This is one of Sir Thomas Tresham's buildings, planned in the shape of a Greek Cross. Destined never to be completed, the New Bield remains unaltered since Sir Thomas's death in 1605, but survives, with the Triangular Lodge at Rushton, as a symbol of one man's religious belief transmuted into stone.

Drive north on the A43, connecting with the A427 via Weldon and on to Oundle, then on to the A605, and follow the signs to Fotheringhay. The castle mound at **Fotheringhay** **3** is a reminder of the last days of Mary Queen of Scots, but Fotheringhay is also remembered as the birthplace of King Richard III. The Church of St Mary and All Saints deserves a visit. Continue north west, following directions on to the A47 via the B671, linking up with the A43. Head south for about two miles and turn right for **Kirby Hall** **4**. One of the finest Elizabethan ruins in England, it was the gardens at Kirby Hall that were widely acclaimed during the 17th century. They were the pride of Christopher Hatton IV, the governor of Jersey. Once he retired to Kirby, he was loathe to leave his garden and on two occasions the House of Lords had to send for him to explain his non-attendance!

Continue to **Rockingham Castle** **5**, built by William the Conqueror, but best known for its part in the bitter struggle between King and Parliament during the English Civil War. Originally a Royalist stronghold, Rockingham was stormed by Oliver Cromwell's Roundheads. The Royalists laid siege to the castle, but its defences held out against repeated assaults. Head south along the A6003 and follow the signs to **Rushton Triangular Lodge** **6**. The building – probably the most unusual folly in the county – stands as a monument to the devout Catholicism of Sir Thomas Tresham, representing the Holy Trinity.

Follow the signs for Rothwell and head W along the A14. Turn left on to the A5199. The road passes close to **Naseby** **7** (signposted after approximately 1 mile), scene of the decisive battle of the English Civil War in 1645. After approx six miles turn right towards Holdenby. At **Holdenby House** ⑧, gardens, a falconry centre and working armoury enhance what was formerly the largest house in Elizabethan England and the prison of Charles I. The trail leads by the front gates of **Althorp House** ⑨, the focal point for the world's attention on 6 September 1997, when Diana Princess of Wales was laid to rest here. It has been the home of the Spencer family since 1508.

Continue along the A428 into Northampton, following the ring road until the Hardingstone A508 turn. Here you will find the second **Eleanor Cross** ⑩. Charing Cross in London was built close to the final resting place of Elaenor's funeral bier before it arrived at Westminster Abbey. The existing Charing Cross is a replica erected in 1863. The A43 north will lead back to Geddington.

OPENING TIMES

Lyveden New Bield, open all year, during daylight. **01832 205358.**

Kirby Hall (English Heritage), open daily 10am-6pm (April-Sept), 10am-5pm (Oct), 10am-1pm, 2pm-4pm Sat-Sun (Nov-March). Closed 24-26 Dec and 1 Jan. **01536 203230**. Admission charge.

Rockingham Castle, open (Easter-Oct). **01536 770240**. Admission charge.

Rushton Triangular Lodge (English Heritage), open daily 10am-6pm (April-Sept), 10am-5pm (Oct). Closed Nov-March. **01536 710761**. Admission charge.

Holdenby House open 2pm-6pm Sun-Fri (Easter-Sept). **01604 584307**.

Althorp open (1 July-30 Aug). Advance booking recommended. Ticket information **01604 770107**.

Hardingstone Eleanor Cross.
(Northampton Borough Council)

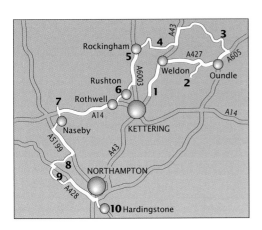

Bolsover Castle.

Rooms
with a **VIEW**

Length: About 75 miles, one/two days

Starting point: Bolsover Castle, Derbyshire

With fabulous vantage points to prospect the lie of the land and lofty views from lighthouses and lookouts, what of the building with no view at all?

Bolsover Castle **1**, with its fairytale appearance, commands spectacular views over the Vale of Scarsdale, and is an impressive sight for passing motorists along the M1, especially at night when it is floodlit. Looking out across the Terrace Range to the far hills, a stunning facade can be seen on the horizon. This is the shell of the 18th-century Sutton **Scarsdale Hall** **2** – and our next port of call. Head back to

Junction 29 of the M1, continuing straight across (not going on to the motorway) and follow the signs for Scarsdale and the signs to the Hall. Needless to say the views back to Bolsover Castle are impressive, too! Head back to the A617 and follow the signs to **Hardwick Hall** **3**. Bess of Hardwick completed the building of the Old Hall in 1591, and it still displays her innovative planning and superb decorative plasterwork. Climb the stairs to the roof level for spectacular views over her country park and 'New' Hall.

Head south along the M1, coming off at Junction 28, following the signs for Alfreton via the A38 and A615. At the junction with the B5035, follow the signs for South Wingfield. Just outside the village is **Wingfield Manor** **4**. Although unoccupied since the 1770s, the manor's 'High Tower' is a testament to Wingfield in its heyday. Immanuel Halton became the first person to view an eclipse of the sun from an observatory here in 1675. Continue along the A5035 towards **Crich** **5**, where there are breathtaking views from the Regimental War Memorial of the Sherwood Foresters. Known as Crich Stand, the memorial is effectively an inland lighthouse. Erected in 1923, the site stands almost 1000ft above sea level and on a clear day Lincoln Cathedral is visible from it. The B5035 now heads towards the northern reaches of Carsington Water. Just before this point, the trail reaches the delightful 'crinkle crankle' wall of **Hopton Hall** **6**, which contains the unusual 'Gell's Tower' – unusual in this instance as the tower is a room with no view at all! Gell's Tower was probably built by Sir Philip Gell, an active and enthusiastic builder in 1790. Sir Philip

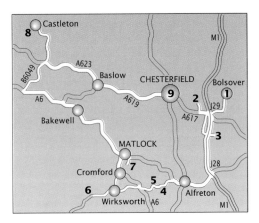

was impatient to get to London, so when the builders came to him for instructions he replied with exasperation: 'Oh, for God's sake go on building,' which they did. When he returned and saw the results of their handiwork he managed, with great equanimity, to accept the situation, muttering: 'Nothing to do now but put a roof on it.' Hopton Hall is now used as holiday homes – the tower is visible, but is not accessible. Head back along the B5035, then north along the B5023 and A6 towards Matlock. In the centre of Matlock, the hills to the east of the town are dominated by the remarkable facade of **Riber Castle** ⑦ – the views looking out from the castle are equally spectacular. The castle can be visited on entering the Wildlife Park that occupies the site. Continue south west along the A6 through Bakewell (perhaps stopping en route for one of Bakewell's famous puddings), heading north along the B6049, which enters the Hope Valley at Castleton.

The remains of **Peveril Castle** ⑧ cannot be missed rising above the town – the steep climb up to the Norman ramparts being well rewarded by the view looking across to Mam Tor and the moors beyond the Derwent Valley, agreed to be amongst the finest views in the Peak District. Head back along the B6049, but this time head east along the A623 and A619 towards **Chesterfield** ⑨. Chesterfield's greatest landmark is undoubtedly the 'Crooked Spire' of St. Mary and All Saints. There are many theories as to how the 228ft spire took its shape, some practical, some not, including lightning strikes, the weight of the devil, and the spire bowing and twisting to admire the beauty of blushing brides!

Peveril Castle.

OPENING TIMES

Bolsover Castle (English Heritage), open daily 10am-6pm (April-Sept), 10am-5pm (Oct), 10am-4pm Wed-Sun (Nov-March). Closed 24-26 Dec and 1 Jan. **01246 823349**. Admission charge.

Hardwick Old Hall (English Heritage), open daily 10am-6pm Wed-Sun (April-Sept), 10am-5pm Wed-Sun (Oct). Closed Nov-March. **01246 850431**. Admission charge.

Hardwick Hall (National Trust), opening times **01246 850430**. Admission charge.

Wingfield Manor (English Heritage), open 10am-6pm Wed-Sun (April-Sept), 10am-5pm Wed-Sun (Oct), 10am-1pm & 2pm-4pm Sat-Sun (Nov-March). Closed 24-26 Dec and 1 Jan. **01773 832060**. Admission charge.

Crich Stand Lighthouse, open 9am-4pm (Oct-March), 9am-5pm (April-Sept) closed Weds. **01773 852350**.

Riber Castle , open all year round 10am-3pm. **01629 582073**.

Peveril Castle (English Heritage), open daily 10am-6pm (April-Sept), 10am-5pm (Oct), 10am-4pm Wed-Sun (Nov-March). Closed 24-26 Dec and 1 Jan. **01433 620613**. Admission charge.

Chesterfield Tower. The Church is accessible 9am-5pm Mon-Sat, Sundays at service times. The tower is open most Bank Holiday Mondays and at advertised times. **01246 206506**.

Sibsey Trader Windmill.

Sentinels of the landscape –
SAILS, STEEPLES AND STUMPS

**Length: About 116 miles,
one/two days**

Starting point: Lincoln

Lincolnshire – flat and bracing, where you can see for miles? In fact, it's a landscape that's full of eye catchers.

Commence at **Lincoln Medieval Bishops' Palace** ❶. Located through the Chesney Gate, literally in the shadow of Lincoln Cathedral, the palace was the seat of religious power between the Thames and the Humber for nearly 500 years. There are spectacular views of the cathedral and over Lincoln. Head out of Lincoln on the A46, turning on to the A17. Follow signs for **Brant Broughton** ❷, where St Helen's church, (grant aided by

English Heritage) has one of the most elegant spires in Lincolnshire, standing 198ft tall. Continue down the A17 passing through Sleaford. The impressive tower visible on the left after a couple of miles is part of the RAF College base at Cranwell.

Approximately four miles east of Sleaford is **Heckington Windmill** ❸. Heckington is unusual as it has eight sails and is in working order. Head out on the B1394 heading east, and then take a short diversion north to South Kyme. The splendid tower (on Church Lane, adjacent to St. Mary's and All Saints) was once part of a castle, built for display rather than defence. The tower is currently grant-aided by English Heritage.

Return back to the A17 and follow the signs for Boston. The famous **Boston Stump** ❹ is a landmark known miles around. The stump is actually the steeple of St. Botolph's Church, which has a step for every day of the year leading up to the top of the tower, which stands 282ft tall. The building of the stump commenced in 1309, and was financed by Boston's then rich wool trade. Head out of Boston on the Grimsby road (A16), passing the **Maud Foster Windmill** ❺. It is recognised as one of the most impressive – and certainly the tallest – working windmill in Britain. Another operational windmill can be visited in Sibsey (follow the signs north along the A16). The **Sibsey Trader Windmill** ⑥ operates on occasional 'Milling Sundays'.

Continue along the A16 to the junction with the A155 and follow the signs to **Bolingbroke Castle** ⑦. Although now a ruin, the Castle was a giant of its day – the birthplace of Henry IV. Fire your imagination and trace out the walls and towers, and visualise Bolingbroke's once majestic appearance. Head back on to the A155 and head west towards Coningsby and Tattershall. **Tattershall Castle** ⑧ is an impressive 100ft high – from its rooftop walkway there are spectacular views over the surrounding countryside, with Boston Stump and Lincoln Cathedral visible on

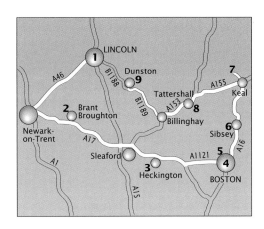

clear days. Continue west along the A155, turning on to the B1189 at Billinghay, travelling through Metheringham on to the B1202, then right on to the A15. A short distance on the right hand side is **Dunston Pillar** ⑨, accessible via a public footpath. Once 92ft tall, the pillar was a guide to travellers, with its beacon reputedly lit straight from hell's fires! The top 60ft of the pillar was removed after the war (including the statue of George III, which can now be seen in the grounds of Lincoln Castle) as it proved a hazard to the RAF. Join the B1188, this road eventually leads back into Lincoln. You cannot miss the spectacular Cathedral dominating the distant landscape.

OPENING
TIMES

Lincoln Medieval Bishops' Palace (English Heritage), open daily 10am-6pm (April-Sept), 10am-5pm (Oct), 10am-4pm Sat-Sun (Nov-March) and daily for Christmas Market. Closed 24-26 Dec and 1 Jan. **01522 527468**. Admission charge.

Heckington Windmill, open 2pm-5pm Sun. **01529 461919**.

Maud Foster Windmill, open all year, 10am-5pm Wed, 11am-5pm Sat, 1pm-5pm Sun, 11am-5pm Thur-Fri (July-Aug). **01205 352188**.

Sibsey Trader Windmill (English Heritage), open 11am-5pm on occasional 'Milling Sundays'. Information **01205 820065**.

Bolingbroke Castle (English Heritage), open daily 9am-9pm (April-Sept), 9am-7pm (Oct-March). Free entry. Site managed by Heritage Lincolnshire.

Tattershall Castle (National Trust), open 10.30am-5.30pm Sat-Wed (April-Oct), 12pm-4pm Sat-Sun (Nov-Dec). **01526 342543**. Admission charge.

Medieval Bishop's Palace, Lincoln.

Castles, retirement homes
AND OTHER PLEASANTRY

Length: Walk A: one mile, about 30 minutes

Walk B: Just over two miles, about one hour 40 minutes.

Walk C: About 1¹/₂ miles, about 45 minutes.

Starting point: Kenilworth Castle, Warwickshire

Explore the most extensive castle ruins in England. Follow our trails beyond the walls to discover a ruined abbey, Henry V's Pleasaunce in the Marsh and Old Kenilworth.

Walk A: Start at **Castle Green** ① in the small car park behind Kenilworth Castle Gate House. Cross the road at the junction and walk on the east side of Castle Road until you arrive at the **Abbey Fields** ②. Take the tarmac footpath, which starts at Ford (Information Board available), and follow across Abbey Fields, alongside Finham Brook, towards the swimming pool. At **Abbey ruins** ③ turn left along the track through the Abbey gateway, then right through the graveyard towards **St Nicholas Church** ④, part of which was rebuilt by Robert Dudley and used by Queen Elizabeth I. Look at the beautifully carved Norman doorway and then take the path up the slope into the **High Street** ⑤ and Old Kenilworth.

Walk B: Start at the castle and follow Walk A as far as the **High Street** ⑤. At the High Street (Information Board available) turn right to the cross-roads, turn right up Bridge Street and Rosemary Hill, past the

Kenilworth Castle.

Theatre **6**, turning right along Abbey Hill. Before you reach the War Memorial, **a row of trees 7** on your right bear plaques to various voluntary organisations. From the **War Memorial 8**, follow along Forrest Road, noticing in the fields to the left, just past the junction with Castle Road, the remains of the castle's **Fish Ponds 9**. Carry on down Castle Road and you will find yourself back at Castle Green and the car park.

OPENING TIMES

Kenilworth Castle (English Heritage), open daily 10am-6pm (April-Sept), 10am-5pm (Oct), 10am-4pm (Nov-March). Closed 24-26 Dec and 1 Jan. **01926 852078**. Admission charge.

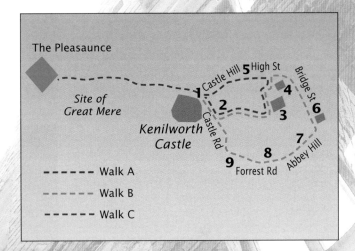

The Pleasaunce

Site of Great Mere

Kenilworth Castle

Castle Hill **5** High St

Castle Rd

Bridge St

1
2
3
4
6
7
8
9

Forrest Rd

Abbey Hill

- - - - - - Walk A
- - - - - - Walk B
- - - - - - Walk C

Walk C: Start from the small car park by the Gate House of the castle. Go uphill to the bend in the road then along Purlieu Lane, first downhill to the Kissing Gate and then uphill to High House Farm. Bear slightly right along a narrow path (which can be muddy and overgrown) and finally over the stile at the end. Immediately in front of you are the remains of the earthworks and dry moats of what was once the timber-framed Banqueting House (the Pleasaunce in the Marsh) built for Henry V following the Battle of Agincourt in 1415. As you return, try to visualise that the area to your right was once the site of the Great Mere, a lake which stretched from the Castle to the Pleasaunce, which in those times could only be reached by boat – and appreciate the superb view of the castle remains in the distance.

Above: The Stables, Kenilworth Castle.
Background: Leicester's Tower, Kenilworth Castle.

Order! Order!

Order!

Length: About 125 miles, one/two days

Starting point: Boscobel House, Shropshire

Medieval Shropshire was home to almost all orders of monks and nuns. But why here, and why are their houses so disorderly now? Hear of miracles and relics, clerical misdemeanours, wine, water, treacery and disaster.

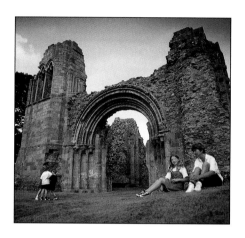

Boscobel House ① **is the modest** country house where Charles II was hidden in 1651 during his flight after the Battle of Worcester, spending one day in the branches of an oak tree to avoid discovery by Parliamentary soldiers. Follow the signs down the lane to **White Ladies Priory** ②, so called because it was the home of reformist Augustinian nuns from the late 12th century. Look out for the graves of the Penderells, the family which hid Charles II.

Return past Boscobel to the A5, and turn left towards Telford. After 4 ½ miles turn right on to the B4379. Just past Sheriffhales, turn left towards Lilleshall – **Lilleshall Abbey** ③ is on your right. Here, a group of canons of the family of Arrouais in north east France settled in 1148 in the wood of Lilleshall. Suppressed in 1538, the west and south sides of the cloister became a private house. The house was fortified during the Civil War and damaged when Parliamentary troops took it by storm. Return to the A5 and turn right and then take the A4422 and A4169 around Telford. At the bottom of Buildwas Bank, turn left towards Much Wenlock. **Buildwas Abbey** ④

Top: Lilleshall Abbey.
Above: Gargoyle at Stokesay Castle.
Right: Wenlock Priary.

is on your right after about 200 yards. Buildwas Abbey, on the south bank of the River Severn, is one of the finest Cistercian ruins in England, and its church one of the most complete.

Leaving Buildwas, turn right on the A4169 to Much Wenlock and follow the signs to **Wenlock Priory** 5, a Saxon monastery for men and women, refounded as a house for Cluniac monks before 1082. Wenlock retains the remains of its late 12th-century cloister laver where the monks washed before meals – look for the carved panels that decorated it. From Much Wenlock, take the A458 to Shrewsbury, and follow the signs for **Shrewsbury Abbey** 6 and the Shrewsbury Quest, home of the fictional brother Cadfael. Built on the site of a Saxon church outside the town, the abbey was established by Roger de Montgomery in 1083. Look for his gravestone and the remains of the shrine of St Winefride, who was brought by Abbot Herebert from Gwytherin in 1137 to provide the growing abbey with its own saint. At the Shrewsbury Quest see brother Cadfael's garden, recreated from the evidence of medieval documents. From Shrewsbury, head north on the A53, turning right on to the B5062, two miles from the city centre.

You will find **Haughmond Abbey** 7 on your left shortly after you cross the A49. Haughmond was a house of Augustinian canons established in about 1135. Best preserved is its 14th-century abbot's house. On the hillside above the abbey, look for the well house that supplied piped water to the abbot.

Return towards Shrewsbury along the B5062 and turn left along the A49 until you come to the A5, which you follow in the direction of Ludlow. The third exit on the left is the A49, signposted for Ludlow and Hereford. Follow this road for 18 miles to Craven Arms. Go through Craven Arms towards Ludlow, and you will see **Stokesay Castle** 8 on your right. Stokesay was the house of a wealthy wool-merchant, Lawrence of Ludlow. Stokesay was 'modernised' in the 1620s – look for its fine parlour fireplace and Jacobean gatehouse.

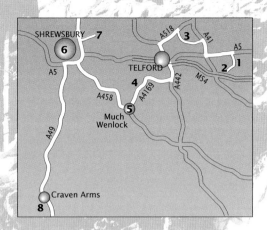

OPENING
TIMES

Boscobel House (English Heritage), open daily 10am-6pm (April-Sept), 10am-5pm (Oct-Nov), Closed Dec-March.
01902 850244. Admission charge.

White Ladies Priory (English Heritage), open any reasonable time. Free entry.

Lilleshall Abbey (English Heritage), open any reasonable time. Free entry.

Buildwas Abbey (English Heritage), open daily 10am-6pm (April-Sept), 10am-5pm (Oct).
01952 433274. Admission charge.

Wenlock Priory (English Heritage), open daily 10am-6pm (April-Sept), 10am-5pm (Oct), 10am-1pm, 2pm-4pm Wed-Sun (Nov- March). Closed 24-26 Dec and 1 Jan.
01952 727466. Admission charge.

Shrewsbury Quest, for opening times
01743 366355.

Haughmond Abbey (English Heritage), open daily 10am-6pm (April-Sept), 10am-5pm (Oct).
01743 709661. Admission charge.

Stokesay Castle (English Heritage), open daily 10am-6pm (April-Sept), 10m-5pm (Oct), 10am-4pm Wed-Sun (Nov-March). Closed 24-26 Dec and 1 Jan. **01588 672544**. Admission charge.

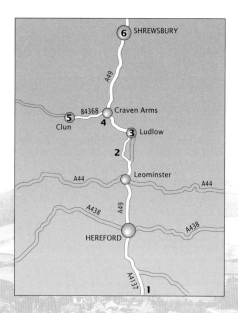

Protecting the KINGDOM

Length: About 65 miles, one/two days

Starting point: Goodrich, Herefordshire

Discover the history of the border between England and Wales – a border which is long and eventful. Explore the Marcher Castles that line the trail, castles such as Goodrich, Ludlow and Stokesay.

Begin at Goodrich (A40 from Ross on Wye or A4137 from Hereford). **Goodrich Castle ❶** is a remarkably complete sandstone castle built on an outcrop high over the Wye Valley. The keep was built in the 12th century and the castle extended in the 13th and 14th centuries. Take the A4137 north (towards Hereford and Leominster) and join the A49, which passes through Hereford (where you

can see Hereford Cathedral and the Mappa Mundi) and Leominster (where you can visit Leominster Priory and adjacent church) and on towards Ludlow. Just before Ludlow visit **Richards Castle ❷**. Follow signs for Richards Castle and turn off on to the B4362 and B4361. The church of St Bartholomew and the much-ruined motte and bailey castle are all that survive of this once prosperous medieval borough. The medieval church and detached stone bell tower are currently being restored with grant aid from English Heritage. The castle can be easily viewed from the churchyard and is in private ownership.

Either rejoin the A49 or follow the B4361 and B4365 north to Ludlow, pausing to admire the dramatic view of **Ludlow Castle ❸**. Ludlow is a planned town within the city walls and has survived remarkably intact. The castle was built about 1085 by Roger de Lacy and by the 17th century, it had become the administrative and judicial capital of the Marches. Follow the A49 north from Ludlow to **Stokesay Castle ❹**. It has been described as the country's finest and most perfectly preserved 13th-century manor house and is set against the backdrop of the Welsh Hills. The superb Jacobean, timber-framed gatehouse gives access to the inner courtyard and the castle's magnificent Great Hall. The adjacent parish church is well worth a visit. Take the A49 north to Craven Arms and turn west onto the B4368 to **Clun ❺**. The Offa's

Above: Goodrich Castle.
Background: Clun Castle.

Stokesay Castle.

OPENING
TIMES

Goodrich Castle (English Heritage), open daily 10am-6pm (April-Sept), 10am-5pm (Oct), 10am-4pm (Nov-March). Closed 24-26 Dec and 1 Jan. **01600 890538**. Admission charge.

Ludlow Castle, open daily 10am-5pm (May-July), 10am-7pm (Aug), weekends only (Jan-Apr, Oct-Dec). Closed Christmas Day. **01584 873947**.

Stokesay Castle (English Heritage), open daily 10am-6pm (April-Sept), 10am-5pm (Oct), 10am-4pm (Nov-March). Closed 1pm-2pm in winter, 24-26 Dec and 1 Jan.
01588 672544. Admission charge.

Clun Castle (English Heritage), open any reasonable time. Free entry. **0345 056785**.

Shrewsbury Castle, opening times information **01743 358516**. Free entry.

Dyke National Trail passes close to the town – a tangible reminder of earlier border disputes. Clun Castle is a spectacular ruin which is best seen from the west. Cross over the River Clun footbridge from the car park and follow the fairly steep winding path up to the keep and towers, passing through the defensive earthworks.

Follow the A488 north to **Shrewsbury** ⑥ and visit its dramatic abbey (home of the fictional medieval monk Brother Cadfael), winding medieval streets and sandstone castle. The town was built within a loop of the River Severn and survives remarkably unchanged from its medieval origins. The well-preserved castle guarded the town against marauders and was built before Domesday. Visitors can now access most of the battlement walkways. The castle, which houses a fine collection of regimental memorabilia, lies immediately adjacent to the railway station.

Steel and stone
AND MILBURGA'S BONES

Length: About 60 miles, one/two days

Starting point: Wroxeter Roman City, Shropshire

We're living in a material world, but did you know how many building materials are in evidence in the West Midlands? There's more than you might think. Discover what events they have been witness to. Walls may have ears – if only they could talk!

Above: Wenlock Priory.
Right: Iron Bridge.
Left Below: Cantlop Bridge.

Wroxeter ① **was the fourth largest** city in Roman Britain, with a huge surviving wall that divided the exercise hall from the baths. See finds from the site in the museum and hear how they have enabled us to reconstruct a clear picture of life 1,000 years ago. Take a cross country route to **Cantlop Bridge** ②, a little cast iron road bridge over the Cound Brook. It was completed in 1812 to designs by Thomas Telford.

Continue south to Acton **Burnell Castle** ③, where you can discover the warm sandstone shell of a moated castle. Here, it is said Edward I held his 1283 Parliament, the first at which 'commoners' were present. A little further south is **Langley Chapel** ④, which has a complete set of early 17th-century fittings redolent with the smell of beeswax polish. The chapel was probably fitted out by the Lee family around 1620, in commemoration of helping King James out of his financial difficulties by purchasing a baronetcy! Continue cross country through Church Preen, Hughley and Stretton Westwood to **Much Wenlock Priory** ⑤. In 1101, when building work was being carried out, bones were located that were believed to be those of St. Milburga. A suitable shrine was built to encourage the development of the priory as a place of pilgrimage.

Now head north along the A4169 to **Iron Bridge** ⑥, site of the world's first iron bridge, spanning the River Severn. The bridge is now a World Heritage Site. Built between 1777 and 1781, it was financed by the ironmaster Abraham Darby. So confident was he of the project that he commissioned an artist so that prints could be produced of the bridge, spreading its fame. One such copy was purchased by Thomas Jefferson and it later hung in the presidential residence in Washington. Return to Wroxeter to complete the circular tour.

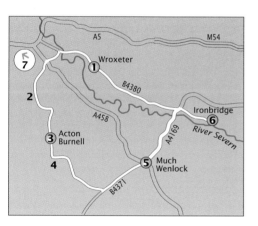

An optional excursion takes in **Old Oswestry Hill Fort** ⑦, a magnificent Iron Age hill fort covering about 68 acres. It is named after the Christian King of Northumbria, Oswald, who was defeated by Penda of Mercia and died nailed to a tree. His martyrdom took place near here and he was later canonised.

OPENING TIMES

Wroxeter Roman City (English Heritage), open daily 10am-6pm (April-Sept), 10am-5pm (Oct), 10am-4pm Wed-Sun (Nov-March). Closed 24-26 Dec and 1 Jan. **01743 761330**. Admission charge.

Cantlop Bridge (English Heritage), open any reasonable time. Free entry.

Acton Burnell Castle (English Heritage), open any reasonable time. Free entry.

Langley Chapel (English Heritage), open any reasonable time. Free entry.

Wenlock Priory (English Heritage), open daily 10am-6pm (April-Sept), 10am-5pm (Oct), 10am-4pm Wed-Sun (Nov-March). Closed 24-26 Dec and 1 Jan. **01952 727466**. Admission charge.

Iron Bridge (English Heritage), open any reasonable time. Free entry.

Old Oswestry Hill Fort (English Heritage), open any reasonable time. Free entry.

Water, water, EVERYWHERE

Length: About 100 miles, one/two days

Starting point: Hatton Locks, near Warwick

H_2O – life-giving, a source of power, a decorative feature, an aid to defence, a cleansing agent and a means of communication. You'll be surprised at how many uses water has been put to in the West Midlands!

Hatton Locks ① are traditionally known as the 'Stairway to Heaven'. They form part of a 21 lock flight that descends 146ft 6ins over a distance of two miles. Travel along the A4177 and follow the signs for **Leamington Spa** ② on the A445. Severn Trent Water welcomes visitors to see how water and sewage is cleaned at a number of visitor centres throughout the region. Find out how ozone is used to make the safest drinking water in Europe at the Campion Hills Water Treatment Works in Leamington. From water as a means of transport and drinking, see how it was used as a means of defence, as well as a food source, at **Kenilworth Castle** ③ – the ruined glory of Elizabethan England.

From Leamington, follow the A452 to the centre of Kenilworth, where signs lead the way to the castle. Kenilworth had water defences from its outset in the early 12th century. Early records show that Henry I's chamberlain, Geoffrey de Clinton, allowed the canons of the priory to fish with nets and boats on Thursdays in the pool beside his castle. Water was important here, both for the monks daily needs and as a means of defence. The castle tour leads out into The Pleasaunce in the Marsh – built for Henry V in 1414, of which earthworks and moats remain. In its heyday, a timber-framed banqueting house stood here in a walled courtyard, surrounded by a concentric water-filled moat that was approachable from Kenilworth's Great Mere. Linking the mere and the Pleasaunce was a water-filled channel, down which the Royal Barge could be sailed or rowed almost direct to the pavilion door. Visitors can still walk out into the Great Mere (dry since Civil War slighting) – and its feeding stream

Above: Witley Court.
Left: Kenilworth Castle.

can be traced through a gap in the dam at Mortimer's Tower (near the ticket point). Another moated site – though here with the moat very much intact – is **Baddesley Clinton** ④. Take the A452 north from Kenilworth, head south along the A4177, then it is signposted after heading north along the A141. The property is little changed since 1634, with priest holes, ponds and a lake walk.

From Baddesley, link on to the M42 heading west, then take the M5 south to junction 5. From here, follow the A38, then A1433 and A433 to Great Witley. **Witley Court** ⑤ is home to the largest stone fountains in Europe. The Perseus and Andromeda Fountain played twice weekly during Witley's heyday under the ownership of the Dudley Family in the 1870s. The fountain was the masterstroke of William E Nesfield, and formed the centrepiece of his Monster Work gardens at Witley. 4,000 gallons of water were pumped from the nearby Hundred Pool to a reservoir over $1/_2$ mile from the house. The water was driven to the fountain by a 40 horse-power steam engine, forming a reported 120ft jet that made the noise of an express train. Now probably the country's finest historical ruin, the Witley fountains are being restored by English Heritage.

OPENING TIMES

Hatton Locks (British Waterways). Information on **01827 252000**.

Kenilworth Castle (English Heritage), open daily 10am-6pm (April-Sept), 10am-5pm (Oct), 10am-4pm (Nov-March). Closed 24-26 Dec and 1 Jan. **01926 852078**. Admission charge.

Campion Hills Water Treatment Works (Severn Trent Water). Group bookings only. Information on **0121 722 4339**.

Baddesley Clinton, open 1.30pm-5pm Wed-Sun (Mar-Oct). **01564 783294**.

Witley Court (English Heritage), open daily 10am-6pm (April-Sept), 10am-5pm (Oct), 10am-4pm (Nov-March). Closed 24-26 Dec and 1 Jan. **01299 896636**.

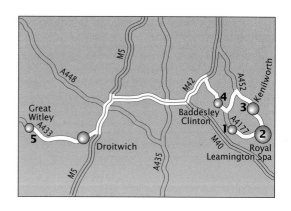

Michael Wood

I come from the industrial north of England and grew up near Maine Road Football Ground, Manchester. My childhood trips were to the Pennines or the Lakes, with holidays on the Yorkshire coast, or in North Wales. It was only later in life that I discovered the joys of East Anglia and gradually came to love the landscape of the East.

Think of East Anglia and you think of flatlands: farm fields stretching from the coast to the Fens; immense skies with puffs of fluffy white cloud; in winter, long strands of frosted poplars towering over wide acres of sugar beet and oil-seed rape. And, to an extent, that picture is true. It is flat, from north **Norfolk** to the Wash and down to **Cambridgeshire**. But what delightful nooks and crannies you will find in the heart of Norfolk, walking Peddar's Way for example, from Wells-by-the-Sea to Boadicea's heartland around Thetford and the Brecklands and the astonishing prehistoric mining landscape of Grimes Graves. Further south, in the Suffolk Wolds, you will find a lovely rolling countryside, going on foot you will soon find mysterious places with medieval churches buried off the beaten track. And let's not forget **Essex** – there are few English counties that are so rich in history, from the lovely old villages of the Colne valley, to Southend with its pier, and its Victorian hotels, to the sombre ring of coastal forts down to Tilbury, which for centuries kept invaders at bay.

My favourite places? That's a hard one! I confess I've a soft spot for the low islands that hug the Essex coast, their tidal creeks thronging with seabirds. And then there's Dedham and Flatford Mill – **Constable country**. Try it at a rooky dusk in November, with the leaves turning gold and you will still feel its magic. Third, I would choose Ely – a haunting place with one of the most beautiful buildings anywhere. Our landscape is one of the things that makes us who we are. And after years of travelling and filming all over the world, what still strikes me about England every time I return is the immense diversity that exists in such a small island. Many such delights are still to be found in the ancient land of the East Angles.

Right: Framlingham Castle; relief carving of king's head.

Fabulous follies and
CENTURIES OF SURVIVALS

Length: About 45 miles, one/two days

Starting point: Audley End House, Essex

The houses of Audley End and Wrest Park are spectacular, but visitors should seek out the gardens to find a treasure trove of historic buildings including pagan altars, Chinese temples and bridges, and upside down memorials. Why were they built? Explore our trail linking the two sites to find the answers and discover other unusual survivals, en route.

The spectacular Jacobean house at **Audley End** ① was described by James I as being, 'too Much for a King, but it might do very well for a Lord Treasurer'. The house itself, with its fine collections, can be visited, but for this trail, it is the unusual garden buildings that are of special interest. At the top end of the park, above the parterre, stands the Temple of Concord. Designed by Robert William Brettingham in 1790, it serves as a premature celebration of George III's recovery from madness. Robert Adam was employed to build a bridge over the River Cam, and later designed the Ionic Temple of Ring Hill to celebrate victory in the Seven Years War. The Tea House Bridge was also constructed by Adam.

From Audley End, follow the signs to **Saffron Walden** ②. Of particular interest are two mazes – a hedge maze in Bridge End Gardens, constructed in 1838/39 and a turf maze – reputedly over 500 years old and the largest example of its kind in Europe. To visit the turf maze, set out from the car park off Common Hill. From Saffron Walden, head north along the B1052, turning left on the A1307, then left on to the A505. After a short distance on the right is a signpost to **Duxford Chapel**, ③ all that remains from St. Johns Hospital, founded around 1200.

Continue along the A505 through Royston – you may wish to track down **Royston Cave** ④, a most unusual survival.

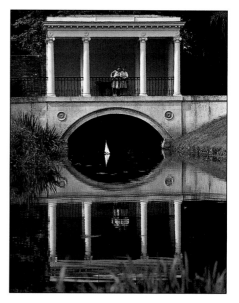

At Baldock, turn north along the A507, continuing until the junction with the A6. Follow the signs to **Wrest Park Gardens** 5. The gardens display over four centuries of gardening styles, laid out before a French-inspired Chateau. The main axis down the garden front centres on a canal, terminating in the Archer Pavilion of 1711/12, which has a fabulous painted interior. On either side of this formality, visitors will be surprised and charmed by garden buildings from the 18th and 19th centuries: the early 18th-century Bowling Green House with its stucco decoration; and the rustic Bath House with pebble pavement and knucklebone floor, representing the late 18th-century taste for picturesque landscape with a Chinese Bridge and a Pagan Altar. The altar was devised by Jemima, Marchioness de Grey, and her husband Philip Yorke in 1748 as a form of intellectual joke. It appears as a three dimensional fiction with a mixture of Greek and Persian inscriptions, and continues to mystify visitors to Wrest Park today! The nearby Capability Brown Column, in recognition of his work at Wrest Park, looks to all intents and purposes as if it has been installed upside down – perhaps another of Philip and Jemima's jokes. They admired Brown's work, but considered him a bit of a 'know-all'.

Left: Audley End.
ow and Background: Wrest Park.

Head west – from Wrest – along an unmarked road to Flitton, where signs will point out the **De Grey Mausoleum** 6. A splendid key gives visitors access to a remarkable treasure-house of funeral sculpture. Possibly the finest tomb is that of Henry de Grey, created Duke of Kent and died in 1740, for whom Leoni re-modelled Wrest Park and Archer created his pavilion.

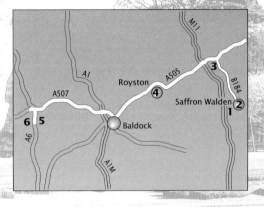

OPENING
TIMES

Audley End (English Heritage), park open 11am-6pm, house open 1pm-6pm Wed-Sun and bank holidays (April-Sept), park and house open 10am-3pm Wed-Sun (Oct). Closed Nov-March. **01799 522399**. Admission charge.

Mazes at Saffron Walden. Information on **01799 510444**.

Duxford Chapel (English Heritage), key keeper's address at site. Free entry.

Royston Cave, open 2.30pm-5pm Sat-Sun (Easter-Sept). **01763 245484**.

Wrest Park Gardens (English Heritage), open 10am-6pm Sat-Sun/Bank holidays (April-Sept), 10am-5pm (Oct). **01525 860152**. Admission charge.

De Grey Mausoleum (English Heritage), open weekends, keykeeper's address at site. Free entry.

Let's find
FLINT

Length: About 82 miles, one/two days

Starting point: Grimes Graves, near Brandon, Suffolk

From deep underground at Grimes Graves, prehistoric miners dug out the largest flint mines in England – a jet black rock with a ready sharp, cutting edge. Tools and weapons were its primary use then, but flint has since been used for some unusual purposes – discover them on our trail!

Grimes Graves.

A 'Flint Trail' could commence nowhere else but at **Grimes Graves** ❶, where flint was extracted some 4000 years ago. Recognised as the earliest major industrial site in Europe, there are about 400 shafts in a 40-acre site, most of which are shallow hollows, giving the impression of a lunar landscape. Visitors can descend 30ft into one of the excavated pit shafts and peer down the radiating galleries.

From Grimes Graves, head south along the A1065 and follow the signs to **Weeting Castle** ❷. The ruins stand in a field beside the church (itself with a lovely flint circular tower) enclosed by a shallow moat. The use of flint in the construction of the castle is clearly visible. A feature of many of the early forts and castles built using flint is the absence of square corners, as unknapped flint is difficult to fashion. While in Weeting, see how flint has been used in the construction of modern bus shelters.

Continue along the A1605 to Brandon. Why not visit the **Brandon Heritage Centre** ❸, in George St, and learn about the gun flint industry? In 1686, a government factory was established at Brandon to produce gun-flints for the army, the contract continuing until the army stopped using flint-locks in the 19th century.

An unusual-looking vicarage can be found at **Barton Mills** ❹, (further south along the A11) where the flint facade blends with yellow brick battlements, creating an eye-catching ensemble. The vicarage can be reached on the far side of the village, past the Post Office and next to the church. Continue south and head for the village of Moulton, where the flint constructed **Packhorse Bridge** ❺ spans the River Kennett. Head east along the A14 to **Bury St. Edmunds Abbey** ❻, where the great west front of the ruins of the church stand in public gardens – early examples of flint masonry. The trail continues along the A134 to Thetford, where **The Ancient House Museum** ❼ (White Hart Street) houses a fine display on flint and its many uses, including display of a flint alphabet. Two English Heritage properties displaying fine examples of flint as a building material can

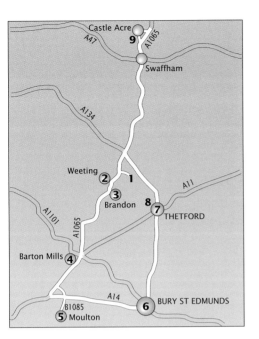

be seen at **Thetford Priory and Thetford Holy Sepulchre** (follow the signs). You can also see how some pre-cast flint panels have been used in the construction of the main shopping centre.

From Thetford, take the A11 and then the A134 towards Dereham. It is worth remembering that men, women and children were employed in the fields round and about to fill buckets with flint stones, which would otherwise cause excessive wear and tear on ploughs and farm machinery. Continue west until the road leads up to the A1065 and follow the signs to **Castle Acre Priory and Castle** . At the priory, visitors are greeted by the remains of a handsome early 16th-century gatehouse of brick and flint. Flint was used as the base for the strong walls of the castle, and can also be viewed on the Bailey Gate between the castle and the priory. In the village of South Acre is a fine example of a flint church. The A1065 leads back to Grimes Graves.

OPENING
TIMES

Grimes Graves (English Heritage), open daily 10am-6pm (April-Sept), 10am-5pm (Oct), 10am-4pm Wed-Sun (Nov-March). Closed 24-26 Dec and 1 Jan. **01842 810656**. Admission charge.

Brandon Heritage Centre, open 10.30am-5pm Thurs-Sat, 2pm-5pm Sun. **01842 813707**.

Moulton Packhorse Bridge (English Heritage), open any reasonable time. Free entry.

Bury St Edmunds Abbey. Information on **01284 764667**.

Ancient House Museum, Thetford, open 10am-12.30pm, 1pm-5pm Mon-Sat, 2pm-5pm Sun (end May-Aug). **01842 752599**.

Thetford Priory (English Heritage), open any reasonable time. Free entry.

Castle Acre Priory (English Heritage), open daily 10am-6pm(April-Sept), 10am-5pm (Oct), 10am-4pm Wed-Sun (Nov-March). Closed 24-26 Dec and 1 Jan. **01760 755394**. Admission charge. Castle Acre Castle, open any reasonable time, free entry.

Castle Acre Priory.

Tilbury Fort.

Pillars and PILL-BOXES

Length: About 53 miles, one/two days

Starting point: Audley End House, Essex

The historic buildings of Essex offer lessons in architectural history; they have also been put to a myriad of surprising uses. The trail acts very much as a beginner's guide to architectural style, with its description of the splendid entrances to Audley End House and Tilbury Fort.

Audley End ① **is one of the great** 'prodigy' houses of the Jacobean period, built in 1605-14 to attract visits from the reigning monarch. At the centre of its fine main frontage lie not one but two entrance porches, creating a carefully-balanced symmetry around the original great hall in the middle. The dual porches provide the key to the original layout of the house, with separate suites of rooms to right and left for use by the King and his Queen, in truly palatial splendour. Porches often provided a focus for lavish detail, and Audley End is no exception. The framework of the design is classical, with superimposed orders, Ionic with heavy spiral scrolled capitals below and Corinthian above. The columns, standing on their pedestal bases and supporting full moulded entablatures (three horizontal members above a column) are set forward from the structure and detached from it, giving depth and interest to the facades. In typical

Jacobean style, the classical form is draped with intricate fretted ornament of Flemish origin, covering almost every available surface (the plainer parapet is a later addition).

This delight in ornamentation even extends to the use of special coloured stones – the columns are variegated, in white marble, black and red, with contrasting elements also picked out in the friezes. This is rich and costly work indeed. During the Second World War, Audley End House served as a secret training station for Polish soldiers of the Special Operations Executive. Further war-time connections can be seen in the grounds. Pill-boxes are a reminder of the GHQ line which extended from Canvey Island to Newcastle, introduced when the threat of invasion was at its peak. Head on to the M11 south and M25, coming off at Junction 30. Follow the signs for Tilbury and later **Tilbury Fort** ➋ (near the docks). The Water Gate at Tilbury presents an impressive show front to the River Thames, a sophisticated piece of architecture quite unlike the more utilitarian character of the rest of the fort.

The restored plaque over the entrance gives the date of its completion: the 34th year of Charles II's reign, or 1683 (measured from Charles I's execution in 1649, and not Charles II's Restoration in 1660). The design of the main fort is by Sir Bernard de Gomme, Chief Engineer and Surveyor General of the Ordnance, but it

seems likely that he received some architectural assistance on the Water Gate. The design, with its central archway and narrower flanks, framed by columns, has echoes of the Roman triumphal arch – an appropriately military theme. Above the Ionic order is superimposed the Corinthian order, with its ornate acanthus leaf carving. To either side are marvellously carved 'trophies' of cannon, armaments and armour, mixing the contemporary with the antique, and serving also to hide the shape of the plain gatehouse behind.

The central niche, now empty, probably once contained a statue of Charles II. Crowning all is an elegantly curved segmental pediment, framing the Stuart Royal Arms. The whole frontage is built of England's finest limestone, brought by sea from Portland on the south coast. In the 18th century, bloodshed took place at Tilbury Fort after a dispute during a county game between Essex and Kent. Feelings evidently ran high, as an Essex man was killed and the fort commander shot dead. Tilbury Fort had been a prison for Scottish soldiers following the Battle of Culloden in 1746. Many prisoners died within the fort or on prison ships bound for the West Indies. The Culloden Memorial Stone stands outside the Water Gate in remembrance of this episode, and the names of the Scottish prisoners who died are held within the fort.

Audley End.

OPENING
TIMES

Audley End (English Heritage), park open 11am-6pm, house open 1pm-6pm Wed-Sun and bank holidays (April-Sept), park and house open 10am-3pm Wed-Sun (Oct). Closed Nov-March.
01799 522399. Admission charge.

Tilbury Fort (English Heritage), open daily 10am-6pm (April-Sept) 10am-5pm (Oct), 10am-4pm Wed-Sun (Nov-March).
Closed 24-26 Dec and 1 Jan.
01375 858489. Admission charge.

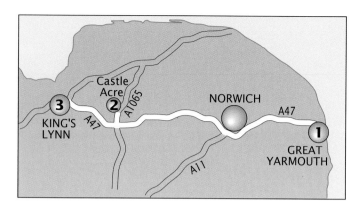

Set sail from the
EASTERN SEABOARD

Length: About 75 miles, one/two days

Starting point: Great Yarmouth

A trail linking the two great seaports of Great Yarmouth and King's Lynn, whose fortunes waxed and waned with trading opportunities between the 17th and 19th centuries. Explore their nautical connections, visiting humble dwellings and rich residences, and follow the trail inland for monastic majesty at Castle Acre.

This trail links the two famous Hanseatic ports of Great Yarmouth and King's Lynn. During the Hanse period, Yarmouth flourished on the strength of the local wool trade and a burgeoning herring industry. For the purpose of the trail, a useful starting point is Row 111

House/Old Merchant's House in **Great Yarmouth 1**, on the South Quay. Here, visitors can experience the contrasting lifestyles of one of Great Yarmouth's wealthy 17th-century merchants and the poorer classes who occupied Yarmouth's unique 'Rows'. Much of this area was destroyed by bomb damage, but the collection of original fixtures and fittings grouped at the properties provides a fascinating insight into the history of the area. Both sites can be visited on guided tours.

While in Great Yarmouth, look out for the town's ancient wall, St. Nicholas' Church, built in 1109 by Bishop Losinga and reputed to be the largest parish church in the country, and the Fisherman's Hospital. Great Yarmouth's most famous resident was Lord Nelson, who has a commemorative 144ft Norfolk Pillar erected in the town. Interestingly, the figure at the top is that of Britannia, not Nelson, and it looks inland rather than out to sea! From Yarmouth, head along the A47. The trail passes close to Norwich, where worsted cloth was once exported into Europe by the boats known as wherries and keels.

Continue along the A47 through Dereham, until you reach the A1065 junction near Swaffham. At this junction

Below: Hanseatic Warehouses, King's Lynn.
Top Right: Old Merchant's House, Great Yarmouth.
Bottom Right: Castle Acre Castle.

OPENING
TIMES

Row 111 House/Old Merchant's House (English Heritage), open daily 10am-6pm (April-Sept), 10am-5pm (Oct), closed 1-2pm. Guided tours. **01493 857900**. Admission charge.

Castle Acre Priory (English Heritage), open daily 10am-6pm (April-Sept), 10am-5pm (Oct), 10am-4pm Wed-Sun (Nov-March). Closed 24-26 Dec and 1 Jan. **01760 755394**. Admission charge. Castle Acre Castle open any reasonable time, free entry.

turn right, then left after a couple of miles, following the signs to **Castle Acre** ②. Both the castle and priory were founded soon after the Norman Conquest of 1066 by William de Warenne, first Earl of Surrey. The priory is the best-preserved Cluniac monastery in the country. Belonging to the centralised order of Cluny, however, did cause problems for the priory when war broke out between England and France in 1295. Edward I took action against the 'alien priories' by confiscating land and thereafter levying heavy taxes.

Head back along the A1065, linking up with the A47 to **King's Lynn** ③. The town was chosen by the Hanseatic merchants as a warehouse base, and was one of England's major ports from the 12th to the 18th centuries. Indeed, the town displays the only remnant of the Hanseatic League in Britain, the Hanseatic Warehouse, and also boasts two superb Guildhalls, the medieval St George's and the chequered-fronted Trinity. Both Guildhalls can be found at the heart of the old town, where Henry Bell's glorious 17th-century Custom House is located, along with the Saturday and Tuesday Market Places.

Let's **look up** in
SUFFOLK

Length: About 37 miles, one day

Starting point: Saxtead Green, Suffolk

If you look up to our ancestors, you'll find they left us much to discover. You may develop a Suffolk stiff neck, but it'll be worth it!

Commence the trail at Saxtead Green **Post Mill** ➊. Look up at the four sails of the mill – the principle of a post mill is that the 'buck' or body of the mill revolves on a post to take advantage of the change in the wind's direction. The interior of the mill displays milling machinery and a fascinating audio tour takes visitors up into the body of the mill and explains the complete milling process. Follow the B1119 a short distance to Framlingham.

From the exterior, **Framlingham Castle** ➋ looks almost as it was when it was built in 1190. It is a magnificent example of a curtain wall castle, with 13 square towers and no keep, showing the influences of the Crusader castles of the Holy Land. If you look up above the walls, you will see numerous decorative brick chimneys, made of specially-moulded bricks in elaborate patterns. Most of them are dummies, put up to give passers-by the impression that this was a great Tudor mansion. Look above the poor house to see five alternate male and female stone heads wearing coronets over the door and windows. If you tour the castle ditches and look up just beyond the bridge columns and to the left of the window openings, a fierce moustached face has been built into the wall. Before leaving Framlingham, be sure to visit the church of St. Michael (visible from the Castle). Look up at its superb roof – one of the most beautiful in Suffolk, with the hammerbeams well concealed by ribbed coving.

Orford Castle ➌ is reached via the B1116, B1078 and B1084. From the outside, look up to see the impressive, near perfect 98ft keep – it has 18 sides and three square turrets, and contains a labyrinth of rooms and passages. Inside the castle, look up in the main chamber – you will see a model of The Merman, a legendary 'Man of the Sea', covered with hair and with a long shaggy beard, who was held captive at Orford. The Merman was allowed to return to the sea, guarded by three lines of nets, but he dived under them to regain his freedom. You'll find another Merman in St Bartholomew's Church in Orford village – if you look carefully! From Orford, head back along the B1084 to **Woodbridge** ➍. The impressive tower of St. Mary stands 108ft tall, with admirably shaped buttresses, crenellations and pinnacles. A short drive along the A12 and the A1214 leads into the centre of **Ipswich** ➎, where the rest of the trail can be followed on foot. The Tudor Christchurch Mansion has collections including Constable and Gainsborough. The Ancient House (dating from about 1670) on St. Stephen's Lane is a superb example of a historic building adapted for various uses over the centuries, with wonderful decorative plasterwork or pargeting. Look up to see four decorative panels representing the continents of Africa, Asia, Europe and America. Cross into Dial Lane and right into Tavern Street. At the junction with St Lawrence Street, look up to see the Ipswich coat of arms, marking the site of Conduit House, where the town's earliest public water supply was piped in. Trace back along Tavern Street to the junction with Cornhill, and look up at the splendid facade of Ipswich Town Hall. Figures on the Town Hall represent Commerce, Justice, Law & Learning and Agriculture (all female), whilst the three portraits are of Richard I, who promised Ipswich a charter, King John I who granted it, and Cardinal Wolsey, one of Ipswich's most famous sons. The female link is restored with figures on the Post Office, representing the Victorian achievements of Industry, Electricity, Steam and Commerce. The Royal Arms can also be seen at Cornhill, flanked either side by Genius and Science – female again! Head south down Princes Street towards the brooding black glass of the Willis Corroon building. Now Grade I listed, the building appears to have a bronze interior at night. The roof actually has a lawn and, if you look up, as well as seeing the sky reflected in the glass, you should be able to make out a hedge running around the roof.

Above: Saxtead Green Post Mill.
Left: The Ancient House, Ipswich.

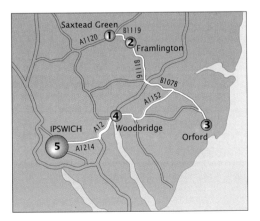

OPENING TIMES

Saxtead Green Post Mill (English Heritage), open 10am-6pm Mon-Sat (April-Sept), 10am-5pm (Oct). Closed 1pm-2pm. **01728 685 789**. Admission charge.

Framlingham Castle (English Heritage), open daily 10am-6pm (April-Sept), 10am-5pm (Oct), 10am-4pm (Nov-March). Closed 24-26 Dec and 1 Jan. **01728 724189**. Admission charge.

Orford Castle (English Heritage), open daily 10am-6pm (April-Sept), 10am-5pm (Oct), 10am-4pm Wed-Sun (Nov-March). Closed 24-26 Dec and 1 Jan. **01394 450472**. Admission charge.

Petroc Trelawny

My walk from home to the BBC may only take 25 minutes, but even that short walk is a daily celebration of London's rich history. I pass a round red brick building in Gloucester Cresent in Camden that was once a leading piano factory, while near the entrance to Regent's Park, there is a grotto honouring a minor saint. The Diorama was a forerunner to the cinema, now the magnificent stucco building is headquarters of the Prince's Trust. Soon after, in Nash's Park Cresent, stands a great granite drinking trough, constructed for the benefit of hungry cart horses. All this in under two miles.

Often I'll head to Soho, its pavement cafes flowing languidly on to the streets. If you blur your eyes, its not difficult to return to more Bohemian days, with artists and writers such as Francis Bacon and Daniel Farson lunching on oysters at Wheelers before losing another afternoon at the Colony Club. At least the French House in **Dean Street** still serves beer in half-pints only, while alongside the sex shops of **Brewer Street,** the Lina store still keeps the best pasta in London and rich smells come from the Algerian coffee roasters in **Old Compton Street.**

When friends come from abroad, I might take them from Tower to Tower, along the banks of the **Thames,** trying to get them to keep their eyes shut until we are on one of the bridges that presents a view of the skyline in all its glory, still dominated by the dome of **St Paul's,** despite the best attempts of this century's architects.

Autumn means heading north to **Hampstead Heath** and its shades of red, brown and gold, the men's and women's and mixed bathing ponds attracting swimmers even in the depths of mid-winter. The problem is that the Heath is high up and offers other vistas of London, more places to go and explore, and with them the realisation that a single human will never discover it all. It may be densely populated, but this city is one of the last places left where we can all be real explorers!

Right: Guilded railings at the Albert Memorial; detail.

Darwin's Rural
RAMBLE

Length: About four miles long, allow at least two hours. There are a few stiles and as it can be muddy when wet;, appropriate footwear is recommended.

Starting point: High Elms Country Park. An alternative is to start from Farnborough Church, which is accessible by bus.

Savour the beauty and tranquillity of the countryside that Darwin knew and enjoyed.

Start from the car park at **High Elms Country Park** ①. Head for the information board and cross the lawn towards the lodge (built by Phillip Hardwick, the creator of the Euston Arch) that guards the main entrance. Cross the road to the footpath opposite and proceed through the wood until you enter an open field with **Farnborough Church** on your right ②. There has been a church on this site since the 11th century, but the present building dates from 1639, when it was rebuilt after a storm. Enter the churchyard and on your right visit the large Celtic cross, the **Lubbock memorial** ③. (If you are starting the trail at Farnborough, the memorial is on your left.) Note the carved image of Avebury circle which Lubbock bought to save it from destruction. An early conservationist, he championed the first laws to protect ancient monuments and took the title of Avebury when he was made a peer in 1900.

Retrace your steps passing the tomb of the legendary **Gypsy Lee** ④. At the churchyard gate, follow the path signposted to Downe. Bear right at the fork, keeping the trees on your right and enter the **wood** ⑤. At the broad path, turn right up the hill to a path on your left which you follow across a field and into a wood. Take the path on the left (marked Farnborough Circular) into an open field. Follow downhill (keeping the trees on your right) until you reach a squeeze stile at the road. Cross to the footpath on the other side, signposted to Downe.

Go through the open field to a path where you turn right (marked London Loop) until you reach a road, where you turn left. A few steps along, pause at the field gate on the right where there is a view of Holwood House on the skyline. Built by Decimus Burton on the site of William Pitt's house, it was here that Pitt and Wilberforce planned the abolition of the slave trade. Continue up the lane, past Penny Cottage, built in 1795, and turn left into Orange Court Lane. At the junction turn left. (At this point the path to your right takes you into Downe Village where you can visit Darwin's home, **Down House** ⑥ a detour which adds about two miles to the walk.)

Follow the path under the power lines to the London Loop path where you turn right. Follow it to the road, enjoying fine views of the valley, originally landscaped by Humphrey Repton to the left, and by Lubbock to the right. At the road, turn left and take the path on the right, which you follow through a wood and across a golf course to another road at **Clockhouse Farm** ⑦. Keeping the farm on your right walk through the orchard to the **High Elms golf course** ⑧. Walk through the car park, aiming for a weeping ash tree where there is a kissing gate and a

Background: Darwin on horseback.
Left Below: The Sandwalk at Down House.

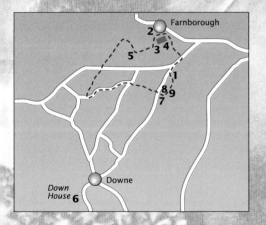

path leading to a yew-lined avenue. At the top of the avenue is a grassy platform, the site of **High Elms Mansion** ⑨ , the former home of the Lubbock family. To your left is the herb garden, to the right an enclosed terraced garden. At the very top is a small summer house built in 1913, a few weeks before Lord Avebury died. Leave the garden by the path opposite the yew avenue and follow it down to the slope, past the former stables – now used as a visitor centre – to the car park where you began the trail. If you started at Farnborough, walk to the lodge and take the path on the opposite side of the road back to Farnborough church.

OPENING TIMES

Down House (English Heritage), open 10am-6pm Wed-Sun (April-Sept), 10am-5pm (Oct), 10am-4pm (Nov-March). Closed February 2000. Groups of 11 or more must book in advance by telephoning 01689 859119. Pre-booking is also required from mid-July to mid-September 2000.

In **the footsteps** of
PRINCE ALBERT

Length: A walking trail less than half a mile long, taking about one hour, but allow more time if you visit the museums. Suitable for disabled visitors.

Starting point: The Albert Memorial

A short walking trail following the life and influence of Prince Albert.

The refurbished Albert Memorial ① was unveiled by Her Majesty the Queen on 21 October 1998 after an acclaimed restoration by English Heritage that took four years and cost £11.2 million. The edifice was to be a lasting emblem of Albert's promotion of the Great Exhibition of 1851 and the subsequent creation of the great institutions which became known as Albertopolis. Standing in front of the Albert Memorial, look across the road to the **Albert Hall** ②. After the Great Exhibition, Albert persuaded the government to purchase a 50-acre site in Kensington. His aim was to develop a series of institutions to promote the study of arts and sciences. At its heart, he supervised the creation of Royal Horticultural Gardens. At its head was to be 'a Great Central Hall'. When laying its foundation, Queen Victoria added the prefix 'Royal Albert'.

The Hall was opened in 1871, ten years after the death of Albert. In 1877, there was a Wagner Festival at the hall conducted by Wagner himself, and in 1912, Sir Edward Elgar, Sir Henry Wood and Sir Thomas Beecham assembled over 500 performers at the Titanic Band Memorial Concert. To the left of the Hall stands **Albert Hall Mansions** ③, where the conductor Sir Malcolm Sargent lived and died. Turn left and walk eastwards towards the Household Cavalry tower block in the distance. Look across to the **Royal Geographical Society** ④, which for over 160 years has been an international focus of geographical research, information and exploration.

Leave Kensington Gardens by **Coalbrookdale Gate** ⑤, made in a foundry in Ironbridge, as an example of the skills of British craftsmen. Note the gilded crowns and VR on the stonework. With your back to the gates, look across the tennis courts to the site of **Crystal Palace** ⑥. It was 562 metres long and 124 metres high, and was built by 200 workers on a platform of concrete that still lies beneath the turf. You can work out where it stood as the concrete has prevented trees planted since 1851 from thriving. Cross the roads to get to Exhibition Road on the south side of Kensington Road and walk down this street.

You will pass a statue of Sir Ernest Shackleton (1874-1922) on the east wall of The Geographical Society.

Walk down the road for five minutes and on your right is **Imperial College 7**, which was created in 1907 from the merging of individual colleges and institutions. **The Church of Jesus Christ of Latter Day Saints 8** was the first Mormon church in London.

The Science Museum 9 has seven floors and more than 40 galleries filled with the world's finest collections in the history of science, technology and medicine.

The Natural History Museum 10 has galleries on dinosaurs, mammals and ecology. Next, you arrive at the **Victoria and Albert Museum 11** . Look for the plaque describing how damage to the walls during the war was left as a memorial to the values of the museum. Turn left into Cromwell Road. The last public act performed by Queen Victoria was to lay the foundation stone of the building that formed the final major addition to the Victoria and Albert Museum. You can see a painting here of the opening ceremony and a model of the Albert Memorial made by the architect Scott to show Victoria his proposed design in 1863.

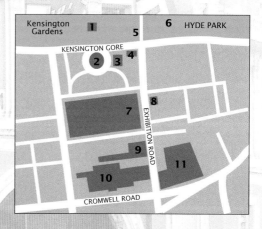

Left: The Albert Memorial.
Below and Background: The Royal Albert Hall.

OPENING
TIMES

The Science Museum, open daily.
0171 938 8000. Admission charge.

The Natural History Museum, open daily.
0171 938 9123. Admission charge.

The Victoria and Albert Museum, open daily.
0171 938 8500. Admission charge.

Romancing the **THAMES**

Length: A walking trail of about 2 – 2 $^1/_2$ miles, one full day.

Information for disabled visitors: The whole trail is feasible for wheelchairs, but the hill up and down to Richmond Terrace is very steep so it might be best not to go right to the top. Wheelchairs can be put on the ferry, but you will need a strong helper to lift you on to the boat.

Starting point: Arrive by tube or train at Richmond-upon-Thames Station.

A day exploring the banks of Britain's most historic river.

Aim to arrive at Richmond Station 1 by 10am, cross the road using the pedestrian crossing and turn left under Orial House down the alleyway. Turn left, and walk past the magnificent **Victorian theatre** 2 designed by Frank Matcham on Little Green. Cross the road to walk diagonally across Richmond Green to the gateway of **Richmond Palace** 3. The fragments here of the outer court are all that now survive of this once magnificent riverside Tudor Palace. You can walk through the gateway (the Private sign applies to vehicles only) into Old Palace Yard and see **The Wardrobe** 4 where soft furnishings were stored.

Trumpeter's House (1702) 5 ahead of you was home to the Austrian statesman Metternich from 1848-51. Turn round and walk back past **Maids of Honour Row** 6 built for Queen Caroline's ladies-in-waiting when she was Princess of Wales to the future George II. Carry on towards Richmond Town Centre. Cross Water Lane to the Old Town Hall. Inside is the **Museum of Richmond** 7, with models of Richmond Palace.

The Riverside Development was designed by Quinlan Terry. Passing the Odeon Cinema, head for Richmond Hill and climb up to the **Terrace** 8 with its celebrated view of the Thames (protected by an Act of Parliament). Walk past the Royal Star and Garter Home for disabled servicemen and women and in **Richmond Park** 9 you have a view of St Paul's Cathedral, 12 miles away. Walk through the park gates, turn right and go through the Pembroke Gardens gate until you reach **Henry VIII Mound** 10 which is the highest spot in the park and may have been a Bronze Age barrow. It is said to be the place where Henry stood when Anne Boleyn was executed. Retrace your steps. Return to the Terrace and walk down through the **Woodland Gardens** 11, with its splendid 18th-century River God. Cross under the road and you will emerge on to the riverbank. Then turn left and walk along the riverbank past Petersham Meadows.

After a few hundred metres you will

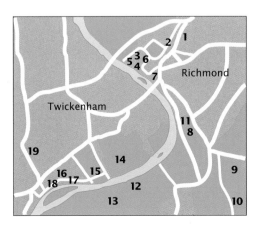

Marble Hill House.

OPENING TIMES

Ham ferry, operates winter weekends, daily in the summer. Charge.

Ham House, (National Trust) open Sat-Wed in the summer. **0181 940 1950.** Admission charge.

Marble Hill House (English Heritage), daily 10am-6pm (April-Sept), 10am-5pm (Oct), 10am-4pm Wed-Sun (Nov-March). Closed 24-26 Dec, 1-18 Jan 2001. **0181 892 5115.** Admission charge.

Orleans House Gallery, open 1-5.30pm Tues-Sat, 2pm-5.30pm Sun/Bank Hols. **0181 892 0221.** Free entry.

come to **Ham** ⑫ , the crossing point for the ferry. You can visit **Ham House** ⑬ . It is the most remarkable Stuart house in the country with rare surviving furniture and textiles. Once you've crossed the river, turn right and walk along the tow path for a few minutes, then turn left into Marble Hill Park. You can walk round to the back of the house and visit **Marble Hill House** ⑭ , built as a retreat from Court life for 'the exceedingly respectable and respected' Henrietta Howard, Countess of Suffolk and mistress to King George II. The charming villa contains a wealth of beautiful furnishings, unique embroidery, historic paintings and antique gilded furniture. Turn left out of the house and follow the path straight across the park and left again into the road. Take the next right into the park surrounding **Orleans House Gallery** ⑮ . The Octagon was designed by James Gibbs in 1720 as a summer house. Leave the park by the entrance opposite the house, turning right and walking carefully along the road past the White Swan Pub.

Take the next right into Sion Road, walking past some fine Georgian houses and then left into the park surrounding **York House** ⑯ . Tradition has it that James, the Duke of York's daughters, the future Queen Mary (1662-96) and Queen Anne (1664-1714) were nursed here as babies. Walk past the cast-iron gentleman's urinal made in Glasgow and on through the sunken garden. Cross the road by the bridge, turning right and walking towards **Twickenham's famous naked lady statues** ⑰ . These were acquired by Sir Ratan Tata, an Indian merchant and former owner of York House. Reaching the river you get views across to Eel Pie Island, home of Trevor Baylis, inventor of the clockwork radio. You can walk through the churchyard of **St Mary the Virgin** ⑱ , where the court painter Godfrey Kneller was churchwarden. Alexander Pope is buried inside the church standing up, as there was no room for him lying down. Exit the churchyard on the far side, walk down Church Street and turn right at the end. Cross the road at the lights and walk down the London Road to **Twickenham Station** ⑲ .

the millennium
TRAILS

Length: A walking trail about two miles long. Allow all day if visits are included. Disabled visitors should note that the hill down to Greenwich is very steep indeed.

Starting point: Ranger's House, Blackheath

Meander through one of London's most beautiful parks and the historic maritime village of Greenwich, enjoying breathtaking views across the Thames to regenerated Docklands and the Millennium Dome.

Ranger's House **1** was purchased by the Earl Chesterfield, one of the great characters of 18th-century society. The house is home to the magnificent Suffolk collection of paintings, which includes full length Jacobean portraits. Leave by the front door and turn left, following the wall and passing a plaque showing the Prime Meridian. You are on the edge of Blackheath, an important muster ground for British armies and the place where Wat Tyler assembled his supporters during the Peasant's Revolt. Turn left at the corner and enter **Greenwich Park 2** through the wrought-iron gate. Take either path on your right, keeping Ranger's Field to the left until you reach the road. Cross and enter the **Flower Garden 3**, passing a sweet chestnut tree planted 1662/4. Where the path divides, take the right fork. Ignore the right turn, then the path drops

downhill slightly. Fork left and then turn right as soon as you reach the lake edge and walk past a heather garden. Keeping left, you exit the Flower Garden with the bandstand opposite. Turn right and follow the path to the junction.

Ahead, in a small wrought-iron enclosure are the remains of a **Romano-Celtic temple 4**. Take the downhill path with chestnut trees either side. Turn first left and walk past 'Queen Elizabeth Oak'. Continue on the same path towards the observatory building and **statue of General James Wolfe** (1727-59) **5**, whose daring attack on the French in Quebec secured Canada for the British. You can take time to visit the **Old Royal Observatory 6** and see the countdown clock to the Millennium.

If you just want to stand astride the **Meridian 7**, walk through the small kissing gate to the right of the magnetic clock. To continue, walk around the back of Wolfe's statue with the iron railing to your right. Turn right after the Planetarium and cross the road, noting the toilets on the right-hand side. Follow the path opposite until you come to the **tumuli**, burial mounds constructed in the Bronze Age **8**.

On your right is the Sir Henry Moore sculpture **'Standing Figure Knife Edge'**

Exit the park gate ahead and follow the gravel path to the road. **McCartney House** ⑩ (former home of James Wolfe) is on your left. Turn right and walk past the White House and descend Crooms Hill. Where it levels out, by the plaque to founder of the NSPCC Benjamin Waugh, turn right into the park again and fork left along the path towards the main entrance.

Walk past a stone statue of **William IV, 'the sailor king'** ⑪ , and turn into the grounds of the **National Maritime Museum** ⑫ . Continue in the same direction along the path. Fork left and walk under the colonnade, which commemorates the Battle of Trafalgar in 1805. Follow the path to walk in front of the **Queen's House** ⑬ , the first wholly classical building in England, designed by Inigo Jones in 1616. With the Queen's House behind you, head for a collection of historic anchors to cross the busy main road at the pedestrian lights. Turn into Park Row and make for the River Thames and **The Trafalgar Tavern** ⑭ , a popular haunt for writers such as Dickens and Thackeray. Walk along the river,

Left: The Royal Naval College from across the Thames.
Below: The Queen's House.

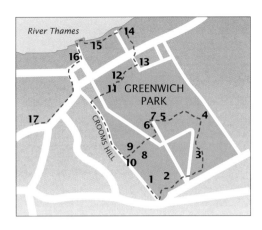

passing the former **Royal Naval College** ⑮ , begun in the 1660s and built on the site of Henry VIII's Palace of Placentia by John Webb (nephew of Inigo Jones), Sir Christopher Wren and Nicholas Hawksmoor. Continue by the entrance to the pier. To your left is the **Cutty Sark** ⑯ , built in 1869 and now the only surviving clipper. Walk along the starboard side of the ship and you will see the entrance to the **Millennium Experience Visitor Centre** ⑰ . The railway station is a five minute walk down Greenwich High Road.

OPENING TIMES

Ranger's House (English Heritage), open daily 10am-6pm (April-Sept), 10am-5pm (Oct), 10pm-4pm Wed-Sun (Nov-March). Closed 24-26 Dec and 1 Jan. **0181 853 0035**. Admission charge.

Old Royal Observatory, open daily. **0181 858 4422**. Admission charge.

National Maritime Museum, open daily. **0181 858 4422**. Admission charge.

Queen's House, open daily. **0181 858 4422**. Admission charge.

Cutty Sark, open daily. **0181 858 3445**. Admission charge.

Millennium Experience Visitor Centre, open daily. **0181 305 3456**.

Tower to TOWER

Length: The trail is less than two miles long and can take anything from three hours to a full day. Most of the trail is suitable for people with disabilities, but wheelchairs would have to detour around the steps down and up from the river. Buggies could be carried up and down quite easily.

Starting point: Jewel Tower, Westminster.

London's High Street is the Thames. Our trail is a photographer's dream, following the river from the Palace of Westminster to the Tower of London.

The Jewel Tower ① was built in 1365 as a personal treasure-house for Edward III and was once part of the medieval Palace of Westminster. Climb up to the road and cross to The Palace of Westminster, which was the main Royal residence until Henry VIII built Whitehall

Palace. By 1550, it had become the regular meeting place of Parliament. The buildings you see today date from after 1834.

Passing by the statue of Richard the Lionheart (1157-99) you can see the public entrance to the House of Commons. Continue to the statue of Oliver Cromwell (1599-1658), who came to power in the English Civil War. By **Big Ben** ②, the bell of the Palace of Westminster's clock tower, cross Bridge Street and turn right to walk on to Westminster Bridge and over the River Thames. When you reach the South Bank Lion, descend the steps to the river bank. Walk past **County Hall** ③, the home of London government from 1900-1986.

Follow the **Walkway** ④, created for the Queen's Silver Jubilee in 1977. **The Royal Festival Hall** ⑤ was built in 1951 as the centrepiece of the Festival of Britain. Pass under **Waterloo Bridge** ⑥, largely built by women during the Second Word War. Passing the **National Film Theatre** ⑦, the National Theatre, the London Television Centre and Gabriel's Wharf, you reach the **Oxo Tower** ⑧. Explore the shopping outlets and be sure to take the lift to the eighth floor where there are spectacular views to the north and south.

Close to **Blackfriar's Bridge** ⑨ is the Doggett's Coat and Badge public house, named after the world's oldest and longest single sculls boat race that takes place

Above: Beefeaters at the Tower.
Below: The Tower of London.
Right: Big Ben.

annually on the Thames. Beneath the massive chimney tower, work is in progress on **Bankside Power Station** 10 , which will house the Tate Gallery of Modern Art opening in May 2000. The spectacular wrought-iron gates of the **Globe Theatre** 11 were made using money donated by countries all over the world. Passing Bear Wharf, the stained glass reminds us that bear baiting took place on this site in the medieval period. If you detour to climb the steps of **Southwark Bridge** 12 and turn right you will find yourself on the site of the **Rose Theatre** 13 , built by Philip Henslowe in 1587. It was preserved in the foundations of Rose Court after a well-publicised campaign and archaeological excavation funded by English Heritage. Walking underneath the bridge there is a delightful depiction of the first ever Frost Fair on the river in 1564. Passing the Anchor, leave the river bank to walk down Clink Street past the **Clink Museum** 14 . Precursors of the Pilgrim Fathers movement were imprisoned in the Clink itself. Stop to

look at the ruins of The Great Hall of Winchester Palace, which was the London home of the Bishops of Winchester from the 12th century until 1642.

The Golden Hinde 15 is a full-sized working replica of Sir Francis Drake's 16th century galleon and has sailed over 140,000 miles. Walk round the boat to the right and you can detour again to visit **Southwark Cathedral** 16 , founded in 860 by St Swithun. Returning to the route, follow the cobbled street past Minerva House and under **London Bridge** 17 . The first bridge was probably built of wood during the Roman occupation. Pictorial records show the medieval stone bridge crowded with timber houses three to seven stories high. Now turn left into Tooley Street. Walk down the pavement until you reach Hay's Galleria where you turn left to rejoin the river and walk past the **HMS Belfast** 18 , the largest cruiser ever built for the Royal Navy. Walk along to **Tower Bridge** 19 , which was opened in 1894 and now houses the Tower Bridge Experience. Cross back to the north bank of the Thames to the **Tower of London** 20 , which encompasses 900 years of dramatic and exciting history. Continue another couple of hundred yards to a second set of steps that follow the moat. When you reach the medieval postern gate, walk under a tunnel. Climbing up the steps, you'll pass a statue believed to be the Roman Emperor Trajan and a section of London Wall, dating from around 200 AD. Use Tower Hill tube station to return to where you started.

OPENING TIMES

Jewel Tower (English Heritage), open all year daily 10am-6pm (April-Sept), 10am-5pm (Oct), 10am-4pm (Nov-March). Closed 24-26 Dec and 1 Jan. **0171 222 2219**. Admission charge.

Royal Festival Hall, open daily. **0171 960 4242**.

Oxo Tower, open daily. **0171 803 3888**.

Clink Museum, open daily. **0171 403 6515**. Admission charge.

Golden Hinde, open daily. **0171 403 0123**. Admission charge.

HMS Belfast, open daily. **0171 407 6434**. Admission charge.

Tower Bridge Experience, open daily. **0171 403 3761**. Admission charge.

Tower of London, open daily. **0171 709 0765**. Admission charge.

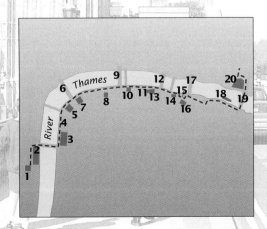

Julian Richards

Despite having spent most of my life as a working archaeologist in landlocked counties such as Berkshire or Wiltshire, I've always been drawn to the sea and it's the coastline of the South East that I find so fascinating.

To me, Bronze Age burial mounds and great prehistoric forts teetering on the edge of high chalk cliffs in **Sussex** are the strongest possible reminder of the irresistible power of the sea. But for thousands of years that same sea has been our last line of defence against threats, both real and imaginary. Walk along any part of the coastline from **Kent** to **Hampshire,** it positively bristles with castles and forts, defensive lines and gun emplacements. Our whole history is there in stone and concrete, from the Roman lighthouse at **Dover** to the desperate defences thrown up in the darkest days of the Second World War.

My own memories are of sunny, rolling cliff-edge downs, where valley follows valley and somehow the beach café is always in the next one over, of windswept visits to huge and rambling forts, and of the ache in the legs from walking the curved shingle spit out into the Solent to Hurst Castle. Today our great coastal defences have become heritage, the conscripts have been replaced by custodians, the gunners by guides and, to my great relief, there's almost always a tea shop.

Right: Upnor Castle's circular staircase.

A **land** rich for
CONQUEST

**Length: About 30 miles, full day
minimum, preferably a leisurely two days**

**Starting point: King Edward's Parade,
Eastbourne, East Sussex**

The South Coast was for long a
target for raiders, conquerors and
settlers. Discover the legacy of these
turbulent times with this trail
around the fortifications and the
battlefield of the victors and
the vanquished.

The Napoleonic Wars (1793-1815) led
to fears of a French invasion. **The
Wish Tower** ① is one of 73
gun-towers, known as Martello Towers built
in order to protect likely landing places in
Kent and East Sussex. On Royal Parade is
the **Redoubt** ②, a circular fort built the
same time as the Martello towers.

Pevensey Castle ③, was the landing
place of William the Conqueror in the
autumn of 1066. It is also one of the Roman
forts of the Saxon shore built to protect
Roman Britain from Saxon pirates. Later, the
castle was refortified at the time of the
Spanish Armada and during the Second
World War. **Battle** ④ saw one of the most
famous military victories in England, when
Duke William of Normandy decisively
defeated the Saxon army of King Harold.
The battlefield and the famous abbey,
founded on the site to commemorate the
victory, can be visited. **Hastings Castle** ⑤
is the site of William's headquarters just
before the Battle of Hastings. Today, you
can see the remains of the early medieval
castle, which throughout its history played a
strategic role in guarding one of the most
important members of the Cinque Ports.

The medieval town of **Winchelsea** ⑥
was built by Edward I as a 'new town' and
is another of the Cinque Ports. As an
important trading port for Gascony wine, this
wealthy town was attractive to raiders from
France. Look out for the town's museum.

Camber Castle ⑦ was built by Henry
VIII in the late 1530s when England was
faced with invasion by the Catholic powers
of Europe. The castle is one mile walk
across the fields. **Rye** ⑧ was a prosperous
Cinque Port that suffered greatly from raids.
Look out for the town walls and great
Landgate that helped protect the town, the
museum in the Ypres Castle and the
Heritage Centre.

Top: The battle of Hastings.
Above: Pevensey Castle.
Right: Pevensey Castle.
Left: The battlefield at Battle.

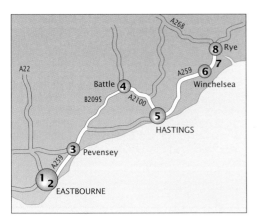

OPENING TIMES

The Wish Tower is now a puppet museum. For opening details **01323 417776**. Admission charge.

The Redoubt is now a museum, open daily 9.30am-4.30pm (Easter-Nov). **01323 410300**. Admission charge.

Pevensey Castle (English Heritage), open daily 10am-6pm (April-Sept), 10am-5pm (Oct), 10am-4pm Wed-Sun (Nov-March). Closed 24-26 Dec and 1 Jan. **01323 762604**. Admission charge.

1066 Battle of Hastings: Abbey and Battlefield (English Heritage), open daily 10am-6pm (April-Sept), 10am-5pm (Oct), 10am-4pm (Nov-March). Closed 24-26 Dec and 1 Jan. **01424 773792**. Admission charge.

Hastings Castle, open all year, for full details **01424 781113**. Admission charge.

Camber Castle, open 2pm-5pm Sat (July-Sept) or monthly guided walks available through Rye Harbour Nature Reserve. **01797 223862**.

St Augustine's Abbey.

A royal
PROGRESS

Length: 25 miles, one day

**Starting point: St Augustine's Abbey,
Canterbury, Kent**

Walk in the footsteps of monarchy
through the ages. Take the trail that
shows you the castles they held court
in, the bed chambers they slept in and
the royal gardens they relaxed in.

Begin at the Abbey ❶, built by St
Augustine and the burial place of
King Ethelbert and Queen Bertha.
Take the Queen Bertha Walk, named in
memory of the Queen of Kent, who kept
alive the flame of Christianity during
England's pagan years until 597 when they
welcomed St Augustine and Christianity
back to Kent.

Take the walk in the direction of the
Cathedral, viewing **the city walls** ❷ and
Burgate ❸, the main medieval street as
you go. **The Queen Elizabeth Tea Rooms**
❹, were reputedly where Queen Elizabeth
met one of her suitors, the Duke D'Alencon
in the panelled first floor room (now a tea
room) when this 15th-century building was
part of the Crown Inn. Travel on to **Dover
Priory Station** ❺. Walk past the building
(now a school and not open to the public),
where King Stephen died – look through
the half arch to the priory. **Maison Dieu** ❻,
was the Court Room founded by Hubert de
Burgh and has connections with Henry III.

Travel up to **Dover Castle** ❼ where,
in the keep, you will be able to witness
scenes of the castle in preparation for the
imminent arrival of King Henry VIII. This
new exhibition depicts the story of events
in 1539 through furnishings, recreated
rooms and interactive displays. Travel on to
Walmer Castle ❽. In this Tudor fortress
turned elegant stately home, Queen
Victoria and Prince Albert stayed in 1842.
Enjoy relaxing in the new garden, designed
and created to commemorate HM Queen
Elizabeth the Queen Mother's tenure as
Lord Warden of the Cinque Ports and to
mark her 95th birthday.

OPENING TIMES

St Augustine's Abbey (English Heritage), open daily 10am-6pm (April-Sept), 10am-5pm (Oct), 10am-4pm (Nov-Mar). Closed 24-26 Dec and 1 Jan. **01227 767345**. Admission charge.

Maison Dieu, Town Hall, Ladywell, Dover, open all year 9am-4.30pm Mon-Sat, 2pm-4.30pm Sun, 9am-4.30pm Bank Holidays. **01304 201200**.

Dover Castle (English Heritage), open daily 10am-6pm (April-Sept), 10am-5pm (Oct), 10am-4pm (Nov-Mar). Closed 24-26 Dec and 1 Jan. **01304 211067**. Admission charge.

Walmer Castle and Gardens, near Deal (English Heritage), open daily 10am-6pm (April-Sept), 10am-5pm (Oct), 10am-4pm Wed-Sun (Nov-Dec, March). Closed 24-26 Dec and Jan-Feb 2000 and when Lord Warden is in residence. **01304 364288**.

Above: Walmer Castle and Gardens.
Background: Dover Castle.

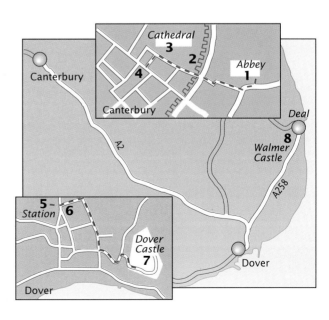

Left and Background: Netley Abbey.

Behind closed
DOORS

Length: About 30 miles, one full day

Starting point: Fort Brockhurst, Gosport, Hampshire

Have you ever wondered how life was for servicemen confined within a 19th-century fort, for wealthy land-owning monks or for farming communities working on the land in Victorian times? This trail gives the opportunity to explore the lives of groups and individuals, both rich and poor, from medieval times to the 20th century, by looking at the places where they lived.

Fort Brockhurst ❶ was one of a line of polygonal forts built in the reign of Queen Victoria to protect Portsmouth, although never fully armed or used for its original purpose. For most of its life, Fort Brockhurst was used for military accommodation. Largely unaltered, the parade ground, the mess, wash rooms and gun ramps can all be viewed.

Travel on to **Titchfield Abbey** ❷, the ruins of an Elizabethan monastery surrounded by a chapter house, dormitory, refectory and kitchen. Medieval monasteries were major landowners and Titchfield had its own farm buildings and large fishpond to supply the canons and novices with food. After the Dissolution, the abbey became the private residence of the Earl of Southampton, who built the two gatehouse towers into the nave of the church. At **Manor Farm Country Park** ❸ the Manor Farm has been home to farming communities from medieval times. Located in a beautiful setting close to the banks of the River Hamble, the farm takes you through the centuries and the lives of those who lived there. Beyond the farm, the park is home to an abundance of wildlife and is designated a 'Site of Special Scientific Interest'.

The **Cistercian Abbey** at Netley 4 was founded in 1239 and colonised by monks from Beaulieu Abbey. The abbey (now in ruins) was built to the standard monastic pattern. It was turned into a private residence after the Dissolution for Sir William Paulet. Netley is a supremely atmospheric site about which romantic poems were written and paintings made in the 18th century. **Medieval Merchant's House** 5 in Southampton is one of the earliest surviving merchant's houses in England. It was both a residence and a business in this lively port, where traders from all over Europe and the Middle East landed cargoes of wine and other goods. Southampton became one of the most important trading ports of medieval England.

In the early 19th century, many large houses were built in Southampton, often in imposing terraces or crescents. A short walk from the centre of the old medieval part of the city, along the **High Street** 6, brings you to this part of the city, much of which has been designated a Conservation Area. Here are the original offices of the Ordnance Survey; the home of General Gordon of Khartoum, and a well-preserved street of artisan's cottages, all with their own story. All these buildings (now privately owned) may be viewed from the street only.

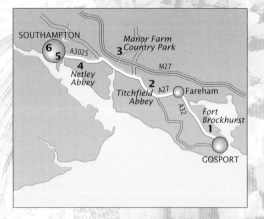

OPENING TIMES

Fort Brockhurst (in Gunner's way, Elson, on the north side of Gosport; English Heritage), open 10am-6pm Sat-Sun (Apr-Sept), 10am-5pm Sat-Sun (Oct). **01705 581059**. Admission charge.

Titchfield Abbey (English Heritage), open daily 10am-6pm (Apr-Sept), 10am-5pm (Oct), 10am-4pm (Nov-March). **01329 842133**. Free entry.

Manor Farm Country Park. Farm open Easter-October. Park open all year in daylight hours. **01489 787055**. Admission charge.

Netley Abbey (English Heritage), open at any reasonable time. **01732 778028**. Free entry.

Medieval Merchant's House (English Heritage), open daily 10am-6pm (Apr-Sept), 10am-5pm (Oct). **01703 221503**. Admission charge.

Fort Brockhurst.

Digging up the
DIRT

Length: five miles, one day. Access for disabled visitors to amphitheatre and Reading Museum only. Footpaths around walls are grassed over and rough.

Starting point: Silchester car park, Hampshire. (Silchester is south of Reading.)

Uncover the fascinating story of Silchester Roman City, from its origin in the Iron Age through its heyday in Roman Britain, and on to medieval and modern times.

From the car park ❶, follow the route-marked path towards the west gate (see orientation panel in car park). You will pass on your left **the section ❷**. The dig in this small section has uncovered both the Roman origins of the site and the medieval buildings that later stood on the site. Then continue along the path, turning right to the medieval church of **St Mary's ❸**. Follow road to the back along a narrow road (caution vehicular access) to the **Roman amphitheatre ❹**. This lay just outside the town walls and could seat over 4,000. Blood-thirsty spectaculars were put on to thrill the audience.

Retrace your steps back to the church and take the **Wall Walk ❺** around the south of the site back to the car park. This will lead you around the best-preserved Roman town walls in Britain. The Museum of Reading has displays relating to Silchester and many artefacts from the archaeological work on site.

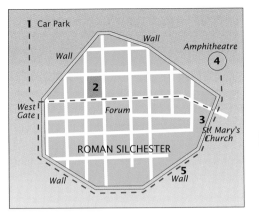

OPENING TIMES

The Museum of Reading, Town Hall, Blagrave Street, Reading. Open all year, 10am-5pm (Tues-Sat), 2pm-5pm (Sun and Bank Holiday Mondays). **01189 399800**.

Left and Below: Reconstruction drawings of Silchester Roman City.
Right: Excavations at Silchester.

Petticoat
POWER

Length: About 35 miles, two leisurely days

Starting point: Osborne House, East Cowes, Isle of Wight

Take an intriguing glimpse into the lives of the powerful and spirited women who made the Isle of Wight their home. Spanning the years and social classes, these women left their own unique mark on history.

At Osborne House ①, **you can visit** Queen Victoria's beloved family home and gardens. View the Royal Apartments and nursery and her private study and bedroom. It was here she died in 1901. Travel on to **Appuldurcombe House** ②. The house (now a shell) was where the illustrious wife of Sir Richard Worsley, Seymour Dorothy Fleming, lived in the late 18th century. She admitted to 27 lovers. At their divorce, her husband failed to win the £20,000 he sought for damages; the jury instead awarding one shilling on the grounds of his connivance. At **Newport Parish Church** ③ you can see the memorial to Princess Elizabeth, daughter of

Charles I, who died from pneumonia at Carisbrooke Castle, aged just 14. Queen Victoria had the monument raised in her memory. In the 13th century, at the age of 25, the young widow, Isabella de Fortibus, last of the de Redvers, found herself sole mistress of one of England's most powerful castles, **Carisbrooke Castle** ④. In an essentially male and hostile world, see the great hall and private chapel (now part of the museum) she built.

In 1896, Princess Beatrice, youngest daughter to Queen Victoria, succeeded to the role of Governor of Carisbrooke Castle, and restored the tradition of being resident at the castle, living there throughout the summer months. **Dimbola Lodge** ⑤, was the former home of Julia Margaret Cameron and is now a museum to the eminent Victorian portrait photographer.

Far Left: Carisbrooke Castle.
Left: Osborne House.
Inset: Appuldurcombe House.
Below: Carisbrooke Chapel.

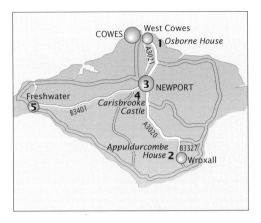

OPENING TIMES

Osborne House (English Heritage), open daily 10am-6pm (Apr-Sept), 10am-5pm (Oct). Winter/Spring tours by pre-booking only **01983 200022**. Admission charge.

Appuldurcombe House (English Heritage), open daily 10am-6pm (Apr-Sept), 10am-4pm (Oct), 10am-4pm Sat-Sun (Nov-Dec, March). **01983 852484**. Admission charge.

Carisbrooke Castle (English Heritage), open daily 10am-6pm (Apr-Sept), 10am-5pm (Oct), 10am-4pm (Nov-March). Closed 24-26 Dec and 1 Jan. **01983 522107**. Admission charge.

Dimbola Lodge, Terrace Lane, Freshwater Bay, open daily 10am-5pm Tues-Sun. **01983 756814**. Admission charge.

Southern Vectis runs a comprehensive bus service on the island. **01983 827005**.

Ferries to/from mainland: Southampton-East Cowes, Red Funnel. **01703 334010**. Portsmouth-Ryde/Fishbourne, Wightlink. **0990 827744**.

Hugh Scully

The South West of England is an ever-decreasing peninsula until, at Land's End, it points its rugged granite finger towards the Atlantic and the New World. The South West is the old world, the part of Britain that sent Sir Francis Drake on his global voyages of exploration, that dispatched the Pilgrim Fathers to America, that waved farewell to the sleek and fast Falmouth Packet ships as they sailed to every corner of the globe and from whence they returned laden with every manner of exotic goods. The South West is all about the sea. **Devon** and **Cornwall, Somerset** and **Dorset,** all come down to meet the ocean and to encounter their history.

Perhaps it is my own deep love of history that makes me very much a man of the South West and why, a few years ago, I decided to return and live beside a Cornish sea. If there is a finer coastline anywhere in the world, I have yet to find it. In the north, steep cliffs battered by fierce winter gales; in the south, meandering river valleys that harbour and protect the richest wildlife; in the middle, bleak moorlands that inspired the novels of Arthur Conan Doyle and Daphne du Maurier; . . . and, off Land's End itself, the romantic home of Wagner's lovers Tristan and Isolde.

The South West is a part of Britain where history, myth and legend have combined into part of the same experience. There is, for instance, the legend that **Tintagel,** on the north Cornish coast, was the site of King Arthur's Camelot. True or false? It hardly matters. The South West, with all its richness and variety, complex textures and scenic splendour is a special place for me.

Right: The sea from Tintagel Castle.

All **roads** lead to
SARUM

Length: About 10 miles, half a day.

Starting point: Stonehenge, Wiltshire

A journey through 5000 years of history from Stonehenge, following in the footsteps of the Celts, Romans, Saxons and Normans at Old Sarum, then on to the superb medieval cathedral at New Sarum – Salisbury.

At Stonehenge, please park in the car park, not on the road verges of the A344. Toilet facilities are available. The great and ancient stone circle of **Stonehenge ❶** is one of the wonders of the world, as old as many of the great temples and pyramids of Egypt. Depart from Stonehenge east bound on the A303 for Amesbury and then follow the A345 for Salisbury and **Old Sarum ❷**. Old Sarum was the original Salisbury. This Iron Age hill fortress was also occupied by the Romans, Saxons and Normans. William the Conqueror built a great palace and the first Salisbury Cathedral here, the remains of which can still be explored today.

Now follow the signs for the city centre into Salisbury. Parking immediately adjacent to the cathedral is severely restricted, but most city parking is within one mile. A parking charge is normally payable. City centre information signing (finger posts) indicate the best ways to reach the cathedral on foot. The medieval **Cathedral ❸** boasts the tallest spire in England and is one of the four surviving originals of Magna Carta. There is much to explore in the historic city of Salisbury, highlights being the Cathedral Close, and for those wanting to find out more about the fascinating archaeology of Wessex, the award-winning Salisbury and South Wiltshire Museum.

Right: Old Sarum.
Below: Stonehenge.
Background: Salisbury Cathedral.

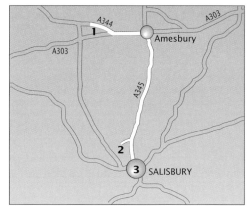

OPENING TIMES

Stonehenge (English Heritage), open all year daily except 24-26 Dec and 1 Jan. For details of opening times **01980 624715**. Admission charge.

Old Sarum (English Heritage), open all year daily 10am-6pm (April-Sept), 10am-5pm (Oct), 10am-4pm (Nov-March). Closed 24-26 Dec and 1 Jan. **01722 335398**. Admission charge.

Salisbury Cathedral, open daily, admission charge applies. For further information on the area, free walks and guided tours leaflets contact Salisbury Tourist Information Centre on **01722 334956**.

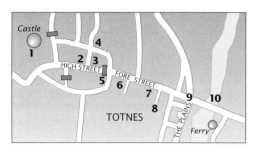

Right: Totnes town and castle.

Map labels: Castle, 1, 2, 3, 4, 5, 6, 7, 8, 9, 10, HIGH STREET, FORE STREET, THE PLAINS, TOTNES, Ferry

Battlements, butterwalks

and BOATS

Length: Totnes town up to two-and-a-half hours with stops, river cruise one-and-a-quarter hours each way plus up to two-and-a-half hours in Dartmouth (including castle visit). Gentle, road walking plus boat trip.

Starting point: Totnes Castle, Devon

A memorable tour of two of Devon's most historic towns, Totnes and Dartmouth, linked by a river cruise through the beautiful scenery of the Dart Valley.

Start your tour with a visit to Totnes **Castle** ❶. The original motte and bailey were planted over part of the Saxon town and defences by a Breton knight called Juhel after the Norman Conquest. Originally consisting of timber buildings, the stone shell keep was built in the early 14th century and from its remarkably well-preserved wall walk, you can pick out the original shape of the medieval town that it dominated. Below the Castle Street entrance, you can see the remains of the medieval North Gate. Walk up Castle Street and turn left into High Street. There are covered walkways on either side that on your right once protected poultry stalls. On the left is the **Butterwalk** ❷, where dairy products, sold from the open-fronted stalls of the Tudor shops, were protected from the sun by the slate fronted accommodation above. The open market place opposite was the site of the flesh 'shambles' where meat was sold.

Continue on down to the parish church of **St Mary's** ❸ on the left. There has probably been a church on this site since Saxon times, but the existing building dates mainly from the 15th century. It also served as the church of the Norman priory behind. Walk through or around to the **Guildhall** ❹ This was originally the priory refectory, but was given to the town by Edward VI for use as a school house and a meeting place for the town's Merchant Guild in 1553. The Town Council still meets here and it is open to the public from Monday to Friday in summer for a modest fee. Turn right and proceed along the cobbled Ramparts Walk, following the line of the medieval town wall, and down the steps to rejoin the street underneath the **East Gate** ❺. This remnant of the old wall was widened for traffic in the 19th century and the building above was badly damaged by fire in 1990, but restored with the help of English Heritage. There are over 60 buildings surviving from the 16th century in the main street alone, many hiding behind modern facades. **The Museum** ❻ building on your right, for example, was built by an Elizabethan cloth merchant and retains its cobbled courtyard behind the former ground floor shop. **The Mansion** ❼, a little further down on your

right is a fine red brick Georgian house and just beyond is **The Gothic House** 8, tucked down Bank Lane and built in 1790 in the distinctive Strawberry Hill style. At the bottom of Fore Street you enter an open area known as **The Plains** 9, with the Royal Seven Stars Hotel on your left. From here cross the bridge 10. This used to be the lowest fording point of the River Dart, which was also navigable for the rest of its length, both major factors in the development of the early town. The converted warehouses once stored food and goods for export down the river. You can follow their scenic route, subject to tides, by taking one of the river cruisers that leave from Steamer Quay down to the historic port of Dartmouth. **Dartmouth** 11 too has its share of historic buildings to explore including another **Butterwalk** housing the town's museum and the splendid St Saviours Church. Whilst there, don't miss the opportunity to stroll out to **Dartmouth Castle** on its beautiful headland or take one of the regular summer foot ferries from the Quay. On the way you will pass **Bayard's Cove Fort**. The castle was built to protect the entrance to the town's busy harbour in the 15th century.

OPENING TIMES

Totnes and Dartmouth Castles (English Heritage), daily 10am-6pm (April-Sept), 10am-5pm (Oct), 10am-4pm (Wed-Sun, Nov-March). Closed 24-26 Dec and 1 Jan.
Totnes **01803 864406.**
Dartmouth **01803 833588.**
River Cruises times, **01803 832109.**

Forts and
FERRIES

Length: one/two days

Starting point: Falmouth, Cornwall

Explore the coastal fortifications that protected the Fal estuary for 450 years. The tour by foot and ferry provides glorious views in an area of outstanding natural beauty.

View over Pendennis Castle towards Fal estuary.

Start your tour at the **Pendennis Castle car park ①**. This vantage point provides magnificent views across the Fal estuary towards St Mawes Castle, which was built by Henry VIII at the same time as Pendennis to protect this strategically important anchorage. Now visit **Pendennis Castle ②**, witness to 450 years of military history (allow 3 hours). Today, Pendennis provides an opportunity to discover the castle's secret past with its re-created First World War guard room, underground tunnels and magazines and special guided tours of the Half Moon Battery – Falmouth's main defence during both World Wars.

On leaving the castle, turn left and walk around the moat, past the HM Coastguard station, responsible for search and rescue for much of the NE Atlantic, to **Pendennis Point ③**. From here, steps lead down to Little Dennis Blockhouse built in the 1540s to provide additional fire-power at sea level. Return to the Pendennis Point car park. To your right a path leads down to Crab Quay Battery, which protected one of the few safe landing places on the headland. The remains of the 17th-century guardhouse and 1902 gun positions can still be seen. Continue along the footpath adjacent to Castle Drive.

You can return to your car or continue down into Falmouth and the ferry to St Mawes. On the way, there is an excellent view over **Falmouth Docks ④**. Falmouth itself only developed in the 17th century, but soon became a major port and principal base for the packet boats that carried mail and passengers all over the world. You pass Arwenack House – former home of the Killigrew family who were captains of Pendennis Castle – and the Custom House, opened in 1814. The ferry from the **Prince of Wales Pier ⑤** to **St Mawes ⑥** takes about 25 minutes.

From the medieval pier in St Mawes, it is worthwhile exploring the side streets that climb the hill of this former fishing village, before following the sea-front road to **St Mawes Castle ⑦**. The castle must be the most picturesque of all of Henry's

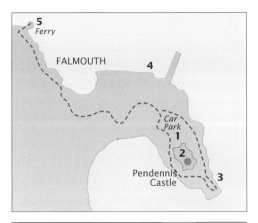

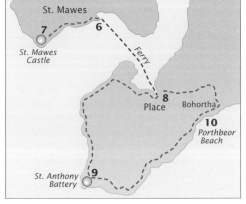

OPENING TIMES

Pendennis Castle (English Heritage), open all year daily 10am-6pm (April-Sept), 9am-6pm July/Aug, 10am-5pm (Oct), 10am-4pm (Nov-March). Closed 24-26 Dec and 1 Jan. **01326 316594**. Admission charge.

St Mawes Castle (English Heritage), open all year daily 10am-6pm (April-Sept), 10am-5pm (Oct), 10am-4pm Fri-Tues (Nov-March). Closed 24-26 Dec and 1 Jan. **01326 270526**. Admission charge.

St Anthony Battery (National Trust), free access at any reasonable time.

Transport Flamouth: Foot, Ferry and Road Train.

Falmouth – St Mawes ferry, daily all year except Sundays in winter. **01326 313201**.

St Mawes – Place ferry, summer only. **01209 214901**.

Falmouth road train. Circular tour connecting Falmouth with Pendennis Castle, summer only. **01872 273453**.

fortifications with its magnificent views, outstanding landscape setting and intricate military architecture. During the summer, you can take the foot ferry from St Mawes to **Place** ⑧ and enjoy the many coastal walks on the Roseland peninsula.

Starting in Place, with its 13th-century church behind the private home of the Spry-Grant Dalton family, a 3 $\frac{1}{2}$ mile circular walk along the coast path takes in the lighthouse built in 1834 and **St Anthony Battery** ⑨. You can visit the restored Battery Observation Post, which plotted the position of enemy ships before following the coast path to **Porthbeor Beach** ⑩. From here, turn left on to a well trodden path across the field. Turn right and immediately left and walk through Bohortha to the far end. Follow the public footpath back to Place.

Pendennis Castle Discovery Centre.

In King Arthur's FOOTSTEPS

Length: 12 miles, up to eight hours with stops, short cut via Bossiney available. Both steep and a little muddy in places.

Starting point: Tintagel, Cornwall

Visit the romantic ruins of the legendary birthplace of King Arthur at Tintagel and experience the dramatic coastline and beautiful countryside which surround it.

From Tintagel village centre, follow **the** sign to the **Parish Church of St Materiana** 1 (approx $^1/_2$ mile). Mostly Norman, the building stands in an early Christian burial ground that may have been the religious centre for the high status occupants of Tintagel Island around the time of Arthur. It also contains a 4th-century Roman milestone found nearby.

Leave the churchyard by the far gate and bear right along a path, following the wall initially. This section of the Coast Path is suitable for wheelchairs and affords good views of the castle. From here on, the path is rough and has steep gradients. Descend to **Tintagel Castle's Barbican Gate** 2. You can rejoin the Coast Path by the English Heritage shop after your visit or continue down the path to the shop without entering the chargeable area. From here on, follow the Coast Path (marked by acorn symbols) to Rocky Valley, taking great care near cliff edges, especially at Willapark, an Iron Age cliff fortress. At **Rocky Valley** 3, you leave it at the

footbridge. Bear right and follow this path by the stream to a ruined mill (beware of loose masonry). Note the Bronze Age carved labyrinths on the rockface to your left. Walk on up to the main road, cross carefully and proceed up the minor road beyond until you reach a footpath sign on left (approx $^1/_4$ mile) just past Halgabron Farm. Climb the stile, cross the field and leave by the kissing gate, descend to the stream, cross the footbridge and bear right, following the path up through St Nectan's Glen to the Hermitage Tea Gardens (approximately one mile). If you wish to see the beautiful waterfall tumbling 60ft into a rock basin or 'kieve' (Cornish for basin) or visit St Nectan's 6th-century shrine, there is an admission charge.

Retrace your steps to the stile near Halgabron Farm, turn left and follow the road for a short distance to a footpath sign on the right, climb the steps over the hedge and proceed across the field towards some cottages. Climb the stile and pass between them, turn right at the road (beware of traffic) and follow for approximately 1000ft before bearing left on to the footpath, over the stile and diagonally across a field and corner of the next field. Continue in a straight line towards some houses. Join the road into Tintagel, left, just before the Catholic Church.

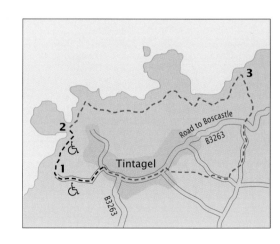

The coast at Tintagel.

OPENING TIMES

Tintagel Castle (English Heritage), open all year daily 10am-6pm (April-Sept), 10am-5pm (Oct), 10am-4pm (Nov-Mar). Closed 24-26 Dec and 1 Jan. **01840 770328.** Admission charge.

King Arthur's Great Halls on the right are open daily (except 25 Dec) and reflect the 1920s romantic view of Arthur and his knights. Admission charge. To finish your tour, a little further on the left is the delightful Old Post Office (National Trust) which was once a manor house and dates from the 14th century. Open daily, April-Oct. Admission charge.

Pilgrims and PUBS

Length: About 80 miles, two days.

Starting point: Winchcombe, Gloucestershire.

A pilgrim's progress to some of the great shrines and public hostelries from the Cotswolds to the Somerset levels.

The George ① was a galleried, courtyard inn (now converted into flats) built for the pilgrims to St Kenelm's tomb at Winchcombe Abbey. **The Abbey** ② was located next to the parish church of St Kenelm. Fragments of it can still be seen in various places in Winchcombe, notably the **Corner Cupboard Inn** ③ on the Cheltenham road. More remains of its great rival **Hailes Abbey** ④, where pilgrims were drawn to view a shrine which housed a phial which was said to contain some of Christ's Holy Blood. Travel on to the Roman city of Glevum, now better known as Gloucester. **The New Inn** ⑤, in Northgate, is close to The Cross, and was built around 1457 next to Gloucester Abbey (now the Cathedral) for pilgrims. It is one of the very best examples of a galleried, courtyard inn in England. The 18th-century appearance of the street front masks a remarkable survival; it is largely timber-framed and on one corner is a rich framework for a much-worn carving of an angel that supports the corner

of the building. Heading south the next stop is the World Heritage Site of Bath. The story goes that the present **Bath Abbey** ⑥ is the result of a dream, when Oliver King, Bishop of Bath and Wells, saw angels worshipping God with the new Cathedral Priory in the background. This is commemorated in the west front carvings and is another good reason to make a visit to this beautiful Georgian city.

From Bath, head for the village of Southstoke, only four miles from the city centre. **The Packhorse** ⑦, the present gabled and mullion-windowed inn, is dated 1674. It straddles the path to the church and is said to be the rebuilding of an earlier inn on the site which, like The George at Norton St Philip, served both travellers to Bath and pilgrims en route to Glastonbury. The bar still opens into the passage through the inn (and still serves good cider).

Another recommended stop is **Norton St Philip** ⑧ and **The George**. This was built, probably, for Hinton Charterhouse Priory close by and patronised by pilgrims to Glastonbury or travellers to Bath. It is one of the great and most outstanding medieval inns in England, stone-built on the ground floor with two oversailing storeys above. The coach arch leads through to a galleried courtyard inside. An interesting detour here is to visit **Farleigh Hungerford Castle** ⑨. The 14th-century chapel of St Leonard boasts wall paintings

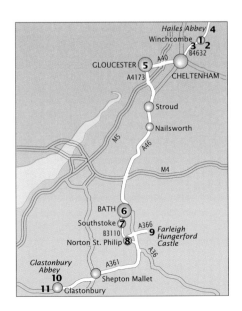

Hailes Abbey.

OPENING
TIMES

Hailes Abbey (English Heritage), open all year daily 10am-6pm (April-Oct), 10am-5pm (Oct), 10am-4pm Sat-Sun (Nov-March). Closed 24-26 Dec and 1 Jan. **01242 602398**.

Farleigh Hungerford Castle (English Heritage), open daily 10am-6pm (April-Oct), 10am-5pm (Oct), 10am-4pm Wed-Sun (Nov-March). Closed 24-26 Dec and 1 Jan. **01225 754026**.

of exceptional richness. The road now continues south to one of the greatest pilgrimage destinations in England, **Glastonbury Abbey** 🔟 , one of the most venerable and perhaps the most famous of England's abbeys. **The George and Pilgrim** ⑪ was built for pilgrims to Glastonbury Abbey, stone-built and with the arms of King Edward IV and of the abbey over the entrance which leads into the stone-flagged passage through the inn.

Sally Magnusson

I live eight miles outside Glasgow, surrounded by fields, with deer nipping across the garden on their way to the forest, and the Campsie Hills close behind. Yet climb the path behind the house at dusk – as I love to do – and look back, and there is Glasgow glittering below you with all its metropolitan seductions a mere 20-minute drive away.

That's what I love about Scotland. Not only can you make a journey of it to revel in genuine wilderness, in the haunting places of the Highlands with their awesome beauty and aching emptiness, but for those like me who want to have their scone and eat it, you are within easy reach of hill and loch and cascading waterfall almost anywhere.

Take **Edinburgh,** where you can be up to your ears and eyes in culture one minute, and striding over the ancient crags of **Arthur's Seat** the next. You can wander down the cobbled **Royal Mile** drinking in centuries of history and then with one turn find yourself gazing out across the North Sea. Where else in the entire world do you get such profligate variety within the bounds of one small nation? From sheer cliff to white beach, undulating hill to gaunt mountain, lush farmland to bare peat-flow. And the water, every sort of water – lochs, burns, gushing falls, great turbulent ocean waves. And the colours: more hues of green in one Hebridean island than you'll see across some whole continents; more purples; more maroons; more shades of pink in the endless skies than Barbie ever dreamt of.

I rave, of course. But then I like the place.

Right: View of Holyrood Park, Edinburgh.

Border ABBEYS

Length: about 30 miles, one day

Starting point: Melrose

This is a compact trail taking you through some lovely Borders countryside and visiting the four border abbeys established by King David I (1081-1153). The abbeys were caught up in the struggles between Scotland and England and were greatly damaged in the many attacks.

In the centre of Melrose is **Melrose Abbey** ❶ where David I introduced the Cistercian order to Scotland in about 1136. The Cistercians were also known as the White Monks, because of their undyed woollen habits. The existing ruins are the result of the 15th-century rebuilding over the ashes of the first church, burnt down by the English King Richard II and his army in 1385. The abbey was again burnt by English forces under Sir Ralph Evers in 1544. Only the commendator's house stands complete, although heavily restored. Melrose has one of the most accomplished collections of medieval carving in Scotland and is also the place where the heart of Robert the Bruce (1274-1329) is buried.

Leave Melrose travelling east and turn right on to the A68 for the two miles to **Dryburgh Abbey** ❷. The abbey was founded in about 1150 under the instructions of the Constable of Scotland, Hugh de Moreville. The Premonstratensian Order, also known as the White Canons, was introduced to Scotland at Dryburgh at that time. This abbey also suffered regular attacks. In 1322, Edward II's army, retreating after an unsuccessful invasion heard the bells of Dryburgh ringing in celebration and turned aside and set fire to the abbey in retaliation. Further devastating attacks took place in 1385 and 1544. Most of what remains at Dryburgh dates to either the early 13th century or to the rebuilding which took place in 1385. After 1600, no canons remained at the abbey and the chapels became private burial places. The two most famous men buried there are Sir Walter Scott and Field Marshal Haig, the commander-in-chief of the British Forces in France and Flanders during the First World War. In 1786, the abbey was bought by the 11th Earl of Buchan who turned it into a magnificent garden ornament, planting trees and shrubs around and within it.

On leaving Dryburgh Abbey, take the B6404 and then left on the B6397 to **Smailholm Tower** ❸. The tower is associated with two noted Border families, the Pringles until 1645 and thereafter the Scotts of Harden, ancestors of Sir Walter Scott. The Pringles built the tower around the middle of the 15th century. The family had been squires to the Earls of Douglas and wielded wealth and influence in the Borders. They suffered heavy losses at the Battle of Flodden in 1513, the Laird of Smailholm losing his elder son and his three brothers. In the 1540's his younger son, John, endured repeated raids by the reivers from Northumberland. Family insolvency led to Smailholm being sold in 1645 to Sir William Scott of Harden, who leased the tower to a kinsman, Walter Scott, the great-grandfather of Sir Walter Scott. In 1773, Sir Walter Scott came to recuperate from a childhood illness at his grandfather's nearby Sandyknowe Farm and it was here that he learnt the tales and songs of the Border countryside from his grandmother and aunt. In 1802, Scott published his collection of stories and ballads, *Minstrelsy of the Scottish Border*. The three upper floors of the tower now house a permanent exhibition of

costume figures and tapestry linking Sir Walter Scott, the *Minstrelsy* and his childhood link with the area. It is only about five miles from Smailholm along the B6397 to Kelso and **Kelso Abbey** 4. This was the earliest of David I's border abbeys, built in 1128. The Tironensian Order, or the Grey Monks, took its name from the abbey of Tiron, near Chartres, which was founded in 1109. The church was built using a very unusual double-cross plan and it was perhaps the most extraordinary Romanesque building in Scotland. Part of the western transept and tower and also the south west corner of the nave still stand to full height. Excavations over the years have revealed an infirmary within the abbey grounds and also the remains of the south transept. Even in its fragmentary state, Kelso Abbey is a superb example of architecture.

The trail now heads south, first along the A698 and then the A68 to Jedburgh, a distance of 12 miles. **Jedburgh Abbey** 5 was established around 1138 for the Augustinian Order, or Black Canons. This order tended to be more adaptable than other orders and the monks, as priests, were often expected to serve the spiritual needs of the layfolk living nearby. In 1296 King Edward I of England lodged in the abbey. Jedburgh suffered even more than the other Border abbeys from attacks from south of the border and it was eventually decided to fortify the abbey. The abbey dominates this Border town with its magnificent west door and the other remains. Alexander III was married here in 1285 and legend has it that a ghostly figure appeared before the congregation at the ceremony and foretold the death of the king. Alexander did die the following year and the succeeding chain of events led to the long and bloody Wars of Independence. Excavations in 1984 uncovered the upper torso of a man who had almost certainly been murdered and also a magnificently carved ivory comb, dated around 1100. Now known as the Jedburgh Comb, it is on display in the visitor centre. The Cloister Garden was recreated in 1986, designed to show how a typical monastery garden may have looked around 1500.

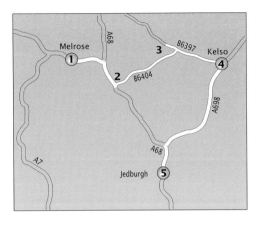

Above: Jedburgh Abbey.
Left and Background: Melrose Abbey.

OPENING TIMES

Melrose Abbey, open all year. **01896 822562**. Admission charge.

Dryburgh Abbey, open all year. **01835 822381**. Admission charge.

Smailholm Tower, open summer only. **01573 460365**. Admission charge.

Jedburgh Abbey, open all year. **01835 863925**. Admission charge.

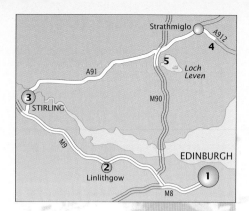

Mary,
QUEEN OF SCOTS

Length: about 73 miles, one/two days.

Starting point: Edinburgh

Mary, Queen of Scots, is one of history's most fascinating figures. Her life contained many elements of high politics, intrigue, romance and tragedy and during her 45 years she was Queen of Scots, Queen of France and some thought she should have been Queen of England.

There are many places in Scotland with connections with Mary, Queen of Scots, but surely the most important place to begin is **Edinburgh Castle** ①. Mary knew the castle well and in 1566 her son, James VI, was born there. This most famous of Scottish castles has a complex building history. The oldest part, St. Margaret's Chapel, dates from the Norman period. James IV built the Great Hall in the early 16th century and the Half Moon Battery was built by Regent Morton later in the 16th century. The castle has a superlative position overlooking the city of Edinburgh and is Scotland's number one tourist venue. Apart from the fabric of the castle and the wonderful views, there is

much to see. The Honours of Scotland are the oldest regalia in the United Kingdom and among the oldest surviving in Christendom. The Sceptre was presented to James IV by Pope Alexander VI in 1494, the Sword of State was presented to James IV by Pope Julius II in 1507 and the Crown was made for James V in 1540. The Stone of Destiny was used for more than 400 years as the seat on which Scottish Kings were crowned. It was removed by Edward I (the Hammer of the Scots) in 1296 and taken to Westminster Abbey in London. The stone was returned to Scotland in 1996, 700 years after it was removed to England. Mons Meg was one of a pair of giant Flemish-built cannons given to James II by the Duke of Burgundy in 1457. The castle also houses the Scottish National War Memorial and the museums of the Scottish United Services, the Royal Scots and the Royal Scots Greys.

On leaving the castle, go to the bottom end of High Street (the Royal Mile) to the Palace of Holyroodhouse, where Mary took up residence after her return from France at the age of 16 to begin her reign as Queen of Scots. At the age of five, Mary had been sent to France and betrothed to Francis, the French king's eldest son. They were married when she was 15 and ruled as King and Queen of France until her husband's untimely death a year later.

We now leave Edinburgh and head west on the M8 and M9 for about 20 miles to Linlithgow and **Linlithgow Palace** ②. This is the birthplace of Mary in 1542. The Royal Palace is now a magnificent ruin set in its own park beside Linlithgow Loch. This was a favourite residence of the Stuart kings and queens from James I onwards at the beginning of the 15th century. Works commissioned by the monarchs can still be seen. The great hall and chapel are particularly fine. Continue on the M9 to **Stirling Castle** ③. This was one of the finest examples of Renaissance architecture in Europe and it is also the royal residence that best represents the Stewart dynasty in Scotland. The position of the castle is very dramatic and it is easy to see how, in days gone by, it was able to control the whole of central Scotland. This meant, of course, that it was in the thick of every major struggle and it changed hands many times in the wars between Scotland and England. The castle sits above two of the most famous battlefields in Scottish history: Stirling Bridge, where William Wallace defeated the English, and Bannockburn, where Robert the Bruce triumphed in 1314 and again established an independent Scotland. Mary, Queen of Scots, gave birth to her son James in Edinburgh Castle, but his baptism took place at Stirling, possibly the first such celebration held in the Great Hall. Taking six months to arrange, the feasting lasted three days and included banquets, spectacles and masques, culminating with fireworks. The Great Hall was again the scene of huge celebrations marking the birth of James VI's son Prince Henry, in 1594. The Great Hall was built by James IV around 1500 and is the largest and finest surviving medieval hall in Scotland, so vast that it has five fireplaces.

The current restoration has recreated the Hall's hammerbeam roof, for which 350 Scottish oak trees were felled. The exterior walls have been re-harled using traditional materials and techniques to recreate them as they would have appeared 500 years ago. Mary, Queen of Scots, was crowned in the Chapel Royal in 1543, when she was only nine months old. The early Renaissance splendour of the Palace is believed to be the work of French masons, brought to Scotland by King James V, who wanted to provide a suitable residence for his second French wife, Marie de Guise. Their daughter was Mary, who spent part of her childhood at Stirling before her marriage to the Dauphin of France.

Below: Edinburgh Castle.
Left: Stirling Castle.

OPENING TIMES

Edinburgh Castle, open all year seven days a week, 9.30am-6.00pm (April-Sept) 9.30am-5pm (Oct-March). Last ticket sold 45 minutes before closing. Closed Christmas Day and Boxing Day. **0131 225 9846**. Admission charge.

Linlithgow Palace, open all year. **01506 842896**. Admission charge.

Stirling Castle, open all year seven days a week. 9.30am-6pm (April-Sept) 9.30am-5pm (Oct-March). Closed Christmas Day and Boxing Day. **01786 450000**. Admission charge.

Lochleven Castle, open summer only. **0388 040483**. Admission charge.

Leaving the castle, take the A91 out of Stirling and head east. Follow this road for almost 20 miles to Strathmiglo and then turn right on to the A912 to Falkland. Here is **Falkland Palace** 4. Far removed from the centres of power, this palace was more of a hunting lodge and was enjoyed by Mary, Queen of Scots. Here she could hunt deer and wild boar in the Forest of Falkland and also indulge in another of her favourite sports, hawking. It is a pleasant palace set in a pleasant village. Retrace your trail to the M90 and head south. At junction 5 you will see Loch Leven, with its castle in the middle of the loch. **Loch Leven Castle** 5 was where Mary was imprisoned after being forced to abdicate by the Lords of Scotland. It was from here that she escaped before her final battle at Langside, outside Glasgow, and was then forced to flee to England and her eventual execution 19 years later.

Above: Dirleton Castle.
Below Right: Edzell Castle.

Historic
GARDENS

**Length: about 127 miles,
one/two days**

Starting point: Dirleton Castle

This is a special trail for gardeners and anyone who enjoys splendid gardens and beautiful surroundings. The distances between the stages are perhaps greater than other trails, but the drive is full of interest, including crossing both the Forth Road Bridge and the Tay Road Bridge.

The gardens we will be visiting in this trail are in the east of Scotland. We will begin at **Dirleton Castle** ①, which is in Dirleton village, three miles west of North Berwick on the A198 from Edinburgh. This is a romantic castle that has often been in the forefront of Scottish history since it was built in the 12th century. The renowned gardens were

devised and laid out in the 16th century by William Ruthven, Earl of Gowrie. The world's longest herbaceous border provides the introduction to this captivating blend of traditional formal gardens and more modern plantings. The gardens at Dirleton emphasise the attraction of this castle, which over the years passed through the hands of three families: the de Vauxs, Halyburtons and Ruthvens. A garden or pleasure ground existed from the time the castle was built in the early 12th century until long after it was abandoned in 1650. The sunken bowling green probably started life as a formally-patterned flower garden surrounded by yew hedges. Beyond lay lawns, specimen trees and an elegant beehive doocot, which provided meat during winter. Historic Scotland has also recreated the Victorian garden devised by the castle's owners in the 1960s.

Travel now towards Edinburgh on the A198 and then circle the city on the A1 and then the ring road A720 to the beginning of the M8. Head for the Forth Road Bridge via the M9 and A8000. Enjoy this crossing of the Firth of Forth and especially the views of the historic Forth Road Bridge, which is a Scottish landmark known throughout the world. At the first junction on the northern side, go right along the A921 to Aberdour and **Aberdour Castle** ②. Aberdour is a wonderful example of how a medieval castle could be extended and modified over several centuries. A castle stood on the site from as early as the 13th century, but the first known mention of a garden is not until 1540. The south terraces were probably laid out by Regent Morton in the 1550s. Detailed plant lists from 1687 include a consignment from the Edinburgh Physic Garden, which notes plums, cherries, jasmine and almonds, among other things. The walled garden was converted into a bowling green by 1668, a use which lasted at least until 1745. This area still abounds with plants which, in season, provide cuttings for sale.

Return now to the M90 and head north to junction eight, where you turn off on the A91 and A92 for Newport-on-Tay and the Tay Road Bridge. On the other side, follow the A90 north, taking you through the pleasant Angus countryside, passing Forfar and Brechin. Just beyond Brechin take the B966 to **Edzell Castle** ③. This is a remarkable and very beautiful complex with a late medieval tower house incorporated into a 16th-century courtyard mansion. The beautiful walled garden is one of Scotland's unique sights, created by Sir David Lindsay, Lord Edzell, about 1604 and recreated in the 1930s. The 'Pleasance' is a delightful formal garden with walls decorated with sculptured stone panels, flower boxes and niches for nesting birds. The chequered arrangement of blue and white lobelia in the wall recesses reflect the heraldic colours of the Lindsays. The decorative hedges are shaped and trimmed into the Fleur de Lys, the Scottish thistle and the English rose and the mottoes of the Lindsay family: *dum spiro spero* (While I Breathe I Hope) and *endure forte* (Endure Firmly). Sir David intended his garden to stimulate both mind and senses. Centuries ago, only the wealthy and secure could afford to create great gardens. Consequently, such designed beauty was as symbolic of personal power as any defensive stronghold. That is the end of our gardens trail but, while you are in the area, why not visit Arbroath Abbey on the coast, the scene of the signing of the Declaration of Arbroath in 1320, which asserted Scotland's independence from England.

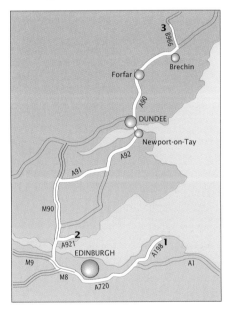

OPENING TIMES

Dirleton Castle, open daily, 9.30am-6.30pm (April-Sept) Mon-Sat 9.30am-4.30pm, Sun 2pm-4.30pm (Oct-Mar). **01620 850330**. Admission charge.

Aberdour Castle, open daily, 9.30am-6.30pm (April-Sept) Mon-Sat 9.30am-4.30pm, Sun 2pm-4.30pm. Closed Thur pm and Fri. **01383 860519**. Admission charge.

Edzell Castle, open daily, 9.30am-6.30pm (April-Sept) Mon-Sat 9.30am-4.30pm, Sun 2pm-4.30pm. Closed Thur pm and Fri. **01356 648631**. Admission charge.

Bishop's Palace.

Prehistoric
ORKNEY

Length: about 42 miles, one day

Starting point: Kirkwall

This is our northernmost trail, which gives insights into life in the islands thousands of years ago as well as more up-to-date sites of historical interest.

We begin at Kirkwall at the **Bishop's and Earl's Palaces** 1. The Bishop's Palace is a hall-house which dates from the 12th century, although it was much altered in later years. One of the changes is a round tower which was built by Bishop Reid between 1541 and 1548. An even later addition was made by the notorious Patrick Stewart, Earl of

Orkney, who built the adjacent Earl's Palace in a splendid Renaissance style between 1600 and 1607. Leave Kirkwall on the A965 and then the A966 and in 17 miles you will find the **Broch of Gurness** 2. A broch is a circular dry-stone tower large enough to serve as a fortified home. They date from the Iron Age. The Broch of Gurness is surrounded by a warren of Iron Age buildings and probably dates to the first century AD. Vikings may have built the long house on top of the ruined broch.

Continue along the A966 and in 10 miles you will come to Birsay. **The Earl's Palace** 3 is the gaunt ruin of the residence of Robert Stewart, Earl of Orkney and was constructed round a courtyard in the late 16th century. Leaving Birsay, take the B9056 to Skaill and here you can visit the 5000 year old village of **Skara Brae** 4 At Skara Brae you can see what life was like in the Stone Age and view houses that were built before the Pyramids and Stonehenge, complete with furniture, hearths and drains. Who lived here? What did they eat? What did they wear? These are the questions that have fascinated visitors to Skara Brae since it was uncovered by a storm in 1850. Find out the answers in the new visitor centre. Interactive displays, original artefacts and an audio-visual

presentation tell the story of the village and its people. A replica house, which visitors can enter to experience life in a prehistoric house, completes the picture. As part of your Skara Brae experience you can visit **Skaill House** 5. This was the home of William Graham Watt, the 7th Laird of Breckness Estate, who discovered Skara Brae in 1850. This important 17th century mansion house was originally built for Bishop George Graham in 1620 and has recently been renovated and opened to the public by the present laird. You will see the Bishop's bed, Captain Cook's dinner service from his ship *The Resolution*, the gun room with sporting and military memorabilia, and many other items collected during the lives of the past lairds who have lived at Skaill.

Drive south to Stromness and spend some time in the town. We are now ready for the last stage of our trail and we head back towards Kirkwall on the A965. In about two miles is **Maes Howe** 6. This is the finest megalithic tomb in the British Isles and was built before 2700BC. The large mound covers a stone-built passage and a burial chamber with cells in the walls. It was broken into in Viking times and runic inscriptions tell of how it was plundered of its treasures by the Vikings.

OPENING TIMES

Bishop's and Earl's Palaces, open daily 9.30am-6.30pm (April-Sept). **01856 871918**. Admission charge.

Broch of Gurness, open daily 9.30am-6.30pm (April-Sept). **01856 751414**. Admission charge.

Skara Brae, open daily 9.30am-6.30pm (April-Sept), 9.30am-4.30pm (Oct-Mar). **01856 841815**. Admission charge.

Skaill House, open daily 9.30am-6.30pm (April-Sept). **01856 841501**. Admission charge.

Maes Howe, open daily 9.30am-6.30pm (April-Sept). Mon-Sat 9.30am-4.30pm, Sun 2.30pm-4.30pm, Closed Thurs pm and Fri (Oct-March). **01856 761606**. Admission charge.

Skara Brae.

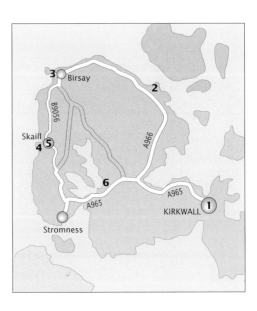

Grampian
CASTLES

Above: Kildrummy Castle.
Right: Huntly Castle.

Length: about 71 miles, two days

Starting point: Craigievar Castle

Aberdeenshire has more castles per acre than any other part of the UK and on your travels along the castle trail, you will pass castles and historic properties at every turning. The trail gives you a selection of castles and grand houses that will give you a flavour of the area and may tempt you to explore further.

From Banchory on the River Dee and only 18 miles from Aberdeen, take the A980 for about 15 miles to **Craigievar Castle** ①. This is Grampian's fairy-tale castle, which exemplifies the best of Scottish baronial architecture. Built by William Forbes in 1626, the castle houses a wonderful collection of family portraits and 17th and 18th century furniture. The house today remains much as it did when lived in by the Forbes-Sempill family.

There are many minor roads to take you to our next stage, but it may be easier to continue on the A980 to Alford, turn left on to the A944 for six miles and then left again on to the A97 for the two miles to **Kildrummy Castle** ②. These are the ruins of a 13th-century stone courtyard castle, which was dismantled after the first Jacobite rising in 1715. The complete layout of domestic buildings is still intact – hall, kitchen and chapel. Kildrummy has been described as the noblest of northern castles and it was a stronghold of the Earls of Mar. Nearby is the Back Den of Kildrummy, now

converted into an attractive garden and spanned by a modern replica of the medieval Brig of Balgownie in Aberdeen.

Head north on the A97 beyond Rhynie turn right on to the B9002 for **Leith Hall** ③. This unusual and attractive mansion house was begun in 1650 with a turreted tower. Subsequent additions have resulted in a house built around a central courtyard. The house contains an exhibition on the military history of the Leith-Hay family and the treasures include the only Jacobite pardon in private ownership. In addition to the house, there are extensive gardens, stables, ponds, countryside trails with bird observation hides, a picnic area and a tearoom. Return to the A97 and drive the few miles to **Huntly Castle** ④. Also known as Strathbogie Castle, this was a former stronghold of the Gordons. This glorious ruin stands on the bank of the River Deveron. It is in itself a history lesson in the development of the Scottish castle from the earliest Norman fortress to the palace of the 17th century. The remains of a 12th-century motte and bailey, a medieval L-plan tower house and defence earthworks of the Civil War are still visible. The most striking features of this palace are the splendid heraldic doorway and the carved fireplaces. Continue north on the A97 for about six miles and then turn right onto the B9024 for Turriff.

Just outside Turriff is **Delgatie Castle** ⑤. This was the home of the late Captain Hay of Delgatie and it was renowned for its painted ceilings, dated 1592 and 1597. The turnpike stair of 97 treads measures over five feet in width. Mary, Queen of Scots, stayed here for three days in 1562. Displays of fine paintings, armoury and Victorian clothes, combined with the atmosphere of a lived-in home, make Delgatie Castle well worth a visit. Some eight miles south of Turriff on the A947 is **Fyvie Castle** ⑥. The five towers of Fyvie Castle enshrine five centuries of Scottish history, each being named after one of the five families who have owned the castle. The oldest part dates from the 13th century and is now probably the grandest example of Scottish Baronial architecture. In addition to the great wheel-stair, the finest in Scotland, there is an exceptionally important collection of portraits, arms and armour and 16th century tapestries. The grounds and Fyvie Loch were designed as a landscaped parkland around the beginning of the 18th century.

On leaving Fyvie, use minor roads to travel the short distance of about seven miles to reach the B999 and **Haddo House** ⑦. It was designed by William Adam in 1731 and the house has always played a special role in local life. Haddo House combines Victorian comfort and Georgian elegance and much of the interior contains fine furniture and ornate plasterwork. The house is bordered by rose gardens and a country park. A few miles to the south on the A920 is **Tolquhon Castle** ⑧. This castle, now a ruin, began life in the 15th century when the Preston Tower was built. In 1420, the Tower passed to the Forbes family and after this date William Forbes, the seventh laird, built a large quadrangular mansion. His stately tomb at the parish church of Tarves is known as Tolquhon Aisle and is situated in the churchyard.

This is the end of our recommended castle trail, but if you have more time to spend in the area, you will find many more historic sites and glorious scenery to delight you. Visit Balmoral Castle and Crathie Kirk, so beloved by the Royal family, and do not forget the many picturesque fishing villages along the Moray coast of Aberdeenshire.

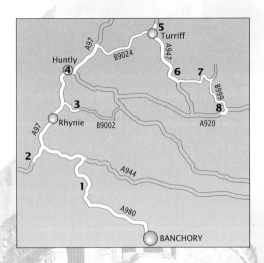

OPENING TIMES

Craigievar Castle (National Trust for Scotland), open daily 1.30pm-5.30pm (May-Sept). Grounds open all year.

Kildrummy Castle, open daily 9.30am-6.30pm (April-Sept). **01975 571331**. Admission charge.

Leith Hall (National Trust for Scotland), open daily 1.30pm-5.30pm (April-Oct). **01464 831216**.

Huntly Castle, open daily 9.30am-6.30pm (April-Sept). Mon-Sat 9.30am-4.30pm, Sun 2pm-4.30pm, closed Thurs pm and Fri (Oct-March). **01466 793191**. Admission charge.

Fyvie Castle (National Trust for Scotland), open daily 1.30pm-5.30pm (21 April-31 May and 1-30 Sept). 11am-5.30pm (June-Aug). **01651 891266**. Admission charge.

Haddo House (National Trust for Scotland), open daily 1.30pm-5.30pm (April-Sept and weekends in Oct). **01651 851440**. Admission charge.

Tolquhon Castle, open daily 9.30am-6.30pm (April-Sept), 9.30am-4.30pm Sat, 2pm-4.30pm Sun (Oct-March). **01651 851286**. Admission charge.

South east
WALES

Length: almost 65 miles, two days

Starting point: Tintern Abbey

A trail which threads its way through the beautiful, wooded and often remote region of the Welsh borders.

Begin the trail at **Tintern Abbey** ① which is only about five miles north of the Severn Road Bridge on the A466. This is the best preserved medieval abbey in Wales and travellers have been coming for hundreds of years to the wooded Wye Valley to admire Tintern's grace and sublime beauty. The abbey was founded in 1131 by the white-robed Cistercian monks. Five miles south of Tintern on the A466 you will come to **Chepstow Castle** ② on its rock above the swirling waters of the River Wye. The building of the castle was started soon after 1067 and it was one of the first stone-built strongholds in Britain. Chepstow grew and adapted over the years and is a history lesson in stone. The castle was in use until 1690 and

Below: Tintern Abbey.
Centre: Raglan Castle.

weathered a long siege in the Civil War.

And now for something different. A little off the A48 are the medieval ruins of Caldicot Castle. It was built along the route of the old Roman road the *Via Julia* which led to the Roman town of Venta Silurum (the modern village of **Caerwent** ③), which is our next port of call. Founded around AD 75 the impressive Roman walls still encircle the area of the town, standing up to 15ft high on the south side. Inside are the excavated foundations of several areas of Roman buildings.

Continuing west along the A48 you will come on **Penhow Castle** ④ just off the main road, some six miles east of Newport. A perfect example of the smaller type of fortified manor house, the main buildings which can be seen by the public are the 12th-century keep tower, the 13th-century curtain wall and the lower hall of the 14th and 15th centuries. Penhow claims to be the oldest inhabited castle in Wales. On leaving Penhow continue west on the A48 to the outskirts of Newport and take the B4236 to the Roman fortress of **Caerleon** ⑤. This is one of Europe's most fascinating and revealing Roman sites. Along with Chester and York this was one of only three permanent bases in Britain built for the elite legionary troops. The Second Augustan Legion stationed here was 5500 strong and a huge military base was constructed to house it. Its Roman name was Isca. The excavated remains give a vivid picture of life in Roman Britain almost 2000 years ago.

Return to the A48 and then turn north on the dual carriageway A449. After 15 miles turn left onto the A40 and follow the signs for **Raglan Castle** ⑥. Dating mainly from the 15th century, in 1646 the castle endured one of the longest sieges in the Civil War before falling to Cromwell's forces and suffering at the hands of his demolition team. Even in ruin, Raglan remains the finest late-medieval fortress-palace in the British Isles and signals the end of an era that began not far away at Chepstow.

The trail now continues along the B4233. From Llantilio Crossenny follow minor roads to **White Castle** ⑦. This little

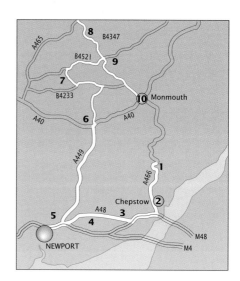

known historical gem is located deep in Wales's border country. This is now a tranquil landscape but in medieval times was hotly disputed territory. White Castle, along with Grosmont and Skenfrith, was one of the 'Three Castles' which were initially built to control a strategic entry point into Wales. When built, the castle was rendered with gleaming white plaster; patches can still be seen.

Take a minor road north to join the B4521 and beyond Cross Ash turn left onto the B4347. We are now going to see the two others in the 'Three Castles' group and in about five miles you will reach **Grosmont Castle** 8. The earliest castle was constructed of earth and timber and the present castle was built in the early 13th century. The name is derived from the French gros mont, big hill, which aptly describes the great earthen mound on which the later buildings stand. The castle saw a great deal of action and Henry III was there in 1233 until he was forced to flee following a daring night attack by Richard de Clare. We are now nearing the end of the trail and the route takes us back down the B4347 towards Monmouth (Trefynwy). In about five miles turn left onto the B4521 where, in a short distance, you will find **Skenfrith Castle** 9, the third of the 'Three Castles'. Originally constructed of earth and timber, it was reconstructed of stone by 1232. In 1201 King John granted the 'Three Castles' to Hubert de Burgh and these strongholds controlled the routes from England into Wales in the gap of fairly open country between the cliffs of the Wye Valley and the Black Mountains to the northwest. In 1239 Hubert de Burgh surrendered the 'Three Castles' to Henry III and they eventually passed to the Earls of Lancaster.

Return to the B4347 and drive the six or seven miles to Monmouth, where you will find **Monmouth Castle** 10 on the western edge of the town. The castle was originally established by William Fitz Osborn, one of William the Conqueror's most trusted barons. The castle was built to command an important double crossing of the Wye and Monnow rivers and the oldest surviving building is the 12th century hall-keep or tower, situated on the west side. On the north is Great Castle House, built in 1673 by Henry Somerset, later the Duke of Beaufort, to replace Raglan as his family's residence in the county following the Civil War. Monmouth is also known as the birthplace, in 1387, of the future King Henry V, victor of Agincourt.

OPENING TIMES

Tintern Abbey, 9.30am-5pm (29 Mar-21 May), 9.30am-6pm (22 May-3 Oct) 9.30am-5pm (4-31 Oct) 9.30am-4pm Mon-Sat (1 Nov-28 Mar) 11am-4pm Sun. Closed 24-26 Dec and 1 Jan. **01291 689251**.

Chepstow Castle, 9.30am-5pm (29 Mar-21 May) 9.30am-6pm (22 May-3 Oct) 9.30am-5pm (4-31 Oct) 9.30am-4pm Mon-Sat (1 Nov-28 Mar) 11am-4pm Sun. Closed 24-26 Dec and 1 Jan. **01291 624065**.

Caerleon Roman Baths & Amphitheatre, 9.30am-5.15pm (29 Mar-31 Oct) 9.30am-5pm Mon-Sat (1 Nov-28 Mar) 12 noon-4pm Sun. Closed 24-26 Dec and 1 Jan. **01633 422518**.

Raglan Castle, 9.30am-5pm (29 Mar-21 May) 9.30am-6pm (22 May-3 Oct) 9.30am-5pm (4-31 Oct) 9.30am-4pm Mon-Sat (1 Nov-28 Mar) 11am-4pm Sun. Closed 24-26 Dec and 1 Jan. **01291 690228**.

White Castle, 10am-5pm (1 May-26 Sept) Winter closed. **01600 780380**.

Above: St Davids Bishop's Palace.
Right: Lamphey Bishop's Palace.

South west
WALES

Length: about 43 miles, one day

Starting point: St David's

Travel from the smallest cathedral city in Britain through the far south west of Wales visiting religious sites and castles, which bring history to life.

The trail begins in St Davids, the smallest cathedral city in Britain, with a population of around 1600. Here, near the centre are **St Davids Cathedral** ① and St Davids Bishop's Palace. St Davids is one of the great historic shrines of Christendom which reaches back fourteen centuries. St David chose this wild, beautiful area as the site of his monastery in the 6th century and you will find his shrine in the purple-stoned cathedral, which nestles inconspicuously in a grassy hollow beneath the rooftops of the tiny city.

In the Middle Ages the bishops of St Davids enjoyed all the trappings of wealth and influence and the most obvious symbol of their status was the great Bishop's Palace. The palace was built in the 14th century and the lifestyle of the medieval bishop is reflected in the extravagance of the architecture. The finest single feature is the Great Hall. This is indeed a fitting place for the shrine of the patron saint of Wales.

Leave St Davids on the A487 for the 16 mile drive to Haverfordwest where, in the centre of the town, you will find **Haverfordwest Castle** ②. From its high vantage point 80ft above the River Cleddau, the castle is a striking landmark which shows how excellent use was made of natural defences in a strategically important area. All the castle masonry is extremely strong and the curtain wall is twelve feet thick on the north west side. The castle was ruined, as were so many others, by the order from Cromwell for its destruction. Just south of the town, on the west bank of the river, is Haverfordwest Priory. Founded by the Augustinians around 1200, little was known of its internal history until recently. Systematic excavation began in 1983 and is now complete and the site is open to visitors. Visitors can see the church, cloister and the rare monastic gardens.

From Haverfordwest travel east along the A40 and off the road in ten miles is **Llawhaden Castle** ③. This was a site of

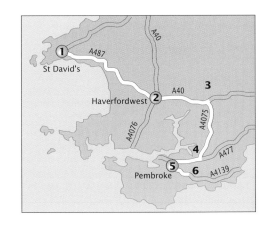

great importance to the bishops of St Davids and lay in the centre of some of their richest estates. The original castle was reconstructed at the beginning of the 14th century as an impressive fortified mansion, designed to provide the residence of a wealthy prelate, quarters for a permanent garrison and lodging for important guests. Return to the main road and take the A4075 south to the junction with the A477 and **Carew Castle** ④. The castle is one of the most attractive in south west Wales and stands above the tidal waters of the River Carew on a low limestone outcrop, with meadows on either side. Carew was built between 1280 and 1310 to replace a more simple Norman structure. The west front is typical of a medieval fortress, with two round towers of immense strength. Their massive spur buttresses, which rise to first floor level, are the most striking architectural features of Carew. The castle was enlarged considerably in the 15th century, when the great hall was built, and the fortress became a fine and comfortable Tudor residence. The mullioned windows are a decorative delight. Near the entrance to the castle stands Carew Cross. This is one of the finest 11th-century crosses in Britain and stands nearly 14 feet high. The swastika and plaitwork patterns on the lower shaft show both Celtic and Viking influence and the wheel-head at the top is fitted into position by a tenon. Today this distinctive wheel-head provides the inspiration for the symbol of Cadw: Welsh

Historic Monuments. Take the A477 west for about four miles and you will reach Pembroke, dominated by **Pembroke Castle** ⑤.

This castle has a long and fascinating history, for it was here that Arnulf of Montgomery built the small inner bailey standing at the end of the promontory. Only a few years later the castle withstood a long siege by the Welsh, although its defenders were near to starvation. The late 12th century keep is both an outstanding feature and an architectural novelty, with its massive cylindrical tower with an unusual stone dome. Views from the top are tremendous and the castle's natural defensive position on a rocky promontory overlooking Milford Haven is immediately apparent. Historically, Pembroke is important not only for its masonry but also the fact that Harri Tudor who became Henry VII and inaugurated the Tudor line of monarchs, was born there in 1457. During the Civil War the castle was attacked in turn by both Royalists and Roundheads as the sympathies of its occupants altered. In the latter stages of the struggle an attacking force was led by Cromwell himself.

And now for a less warlike experience! Leaving Pembroke on the A4139 you will reach Lamphey in no more than two miles and there you will experience the peace of **Lamphey Bishop's Palace** ⑥. Here the medieval bishops of St Davids built for themselves a magnificent retreat away from the worries of Church and State, in which they could combine the life of a prelate with that of a country gentleman. The palace is mainly the work of Henry de Gower, Bishop of St Davids from 1328 to 1347, who was also largely responsible for St Davids Bishop's Palace. The impressive Great Hall is over 70ft long and it is interesting to note the lofty arcaded parapets, an architectural device used also to good effect at St Davids. The palace was surrounded by fishponds, fruit orchards, vegetable gardens and sweeping parklands.

OPENING TIMES

St Davids Bishop's Palace, open 9.30am-5pm (29 Mar-21 May), 9.30am-6pm (22 May-3 Oct). 9.30am-5pm (4-31 Oct) 9.30am-4pm Mon-Sat (1 Nov-28 Mar) 12 noon-2pm Sun. Closed 24-26 Dec and 1 Jan. **01437 720517**.

Lamphey Bishop's Palace, open all year 10am-5pm daily. Closed 25 Dec. **01646 672224**.

Above: Caernarfon Castle.
Right: Plas Mawr.

Snowdonia &
NORTH WEST WALES

Length: about 78 miles, two days.

Starting Point: Conwy

A journey through the mountainous region of Gwynedd with views of Conwy Bay, Cardigan Bay and Snowdon.

Conwy Castle 1 **is a gritty, dark-** stoned fortress which has the rare ability to evoke an authentic medieval atmosphere. It was constructed by the English King Edward I between 1283 and 1289 as one of the key fortresses in his 'iron ring' of castles to contain the Welsh. Its massive military strength springs from the rock on which it stands and seems to grow naturally. Soaring curtain walls and eight huge round towers give the castle an intimidatory presence undimmed by the passage of time. The views from the battlements are breathtaking looking out across mountains and sea and down to the roofless shell of the castle's 125ft hall range. Conwy is the classic walled town and its ring of walls, over 3/4 mile long and guarded by 21 towers and three original

gateways dating from the 13th century, is one of the finest in the world. In the narrow streets at the heart of the town stands **Plas Mawr** 2, an architectural gem which is the finest surviving town house of the Elizabethan era to be found anywhere in Britain. The house is especially noted for the quality and quantity of its ornamental plasterwork. Visitors can take an audio-tour of the house, describing the restoration and the life of the Tudor gentry and servants.

From Conwy the A55 will take you to Bangor where you will find **Penrhyn Castle** 3 just east of the town. A sumptuously appointed residence, Penrhyn was built for the slate baron, G.H. Dawkins Pennant. Exterior and interior are both magnificent and the castle's location in grounds overlooking the Menai Strait complements a lavish, no-expense-spared interior. Slate is used throughout the house – entwined dolphin supports for the large side table in the Great Hall, a full-sized billiard table in the library and even a bed – all made of slate. The bed weighs over a ton!

Now turn onto the B4366 towards Caernarfon and then left again onto the B4547. When you reach the A4086 turn left and in about two miles you will arrive at **Dolbadarn Castle** 4. This castle of the Welsh princes lies in a wild landscape of breathtaking grandeur. The earliest buildings date from soon after 1200, but it is the circular tower that is the dominating feature. The tower is traditionally the place where Owain Goch was imprisoned by his brother, Llywelyn the Last. Now retrace your route west along the A4086 to Caernarfon. As you reach the town you will come on **Segontium Roman Fort** 5. The fort dates back to AD77 when Gnaeus Julius Agricola completed the Roman conquest of Wales by capturing the Isle of Anglesey. It is well preserved and is the only site in Wales where it is possible to see something of the internal layout of a Roman fort. It was garrisoned from AD77 until AD394.

Continue into the town to **Caernarfon Castle** 6. This is possibly the most famous of Wales's castles and its sheer scale and commanding presence set it apart from the rest. Begun in 1283 as the definitive chapter in the conquest of Wales by Edward I, Caernarfon was constructed not only as a military stronghold but also as a seat of government and royal palace. Edward's son, the first English Prince of Wales, was born here in 1284 and in 1969 it was the setting for the Investiture of Prince Charles as Prince of Wales. Caernarfon's position of pre-eminence in the historic rankings is recognised in its status as a World Heritage inscribed site.

Leaving Caernarfon on the A487 there is a 16 mile drive, coming off on the B4411 to **Criccieth Castle** ⑦. Criccieth's history is deeply entwined in the medieval conflict between Wales and England. Originally a stronghold of the native Welsh princes, it was later annexed and added to by the English King Edward I. The castle has a strategic position on a rocky peninsula overlooking Tremadog Bay. It was built by Llywelyn the Great between 1230 and 1240.

Leaving Criccieth take the A487 and A496 to Blaenau Ffestiniog and about 5 miles further on is **Dolwyddelan Castle** ⑧. Dolwyddelan was built as a fortress of the native Welsh princes. The castle occupies a magnificent location deep in Snowdonia, on a ridge set against the rugged backcloth of Moel Siabod. It was built between 1210 and 1240 by Wales's most powerful medieval prince, Llywelyn the Great, ruler of Snowdonia, and it controlled a strategic pass through his mountainous kingdom. A visit to this solitary sentinel is worth it for the views alone – the sweeping mountain vistas visible are truly stunning.

Heading north on the A470, about six miles beyond Dolwyddelan, off a minor road, is **Capel Garmon Burial Chamber** ⑨. This is a well-preserved Neolithic tomb, which dates back to 3500 BC and was excavated in 1924. Some four miles further on, just before Llanrwst, is **Gwydir Uchaf Chapel** ⑩. This lovely little structure was built in 1673 as the private place of worship for Gwydir Uchaf House. The chapel is notable for its contemporary painted ceiling inspired by high Anglican or Roman Catholic liturgical tradition. This ends our trail with a journey of eleven miles to Conwy.

OPENING TIMES

Conwy Castle, 9.30am-5pm (29 Mar-21 May). 9.30am-6pm (22 May-3 Oct) 9.30am-5pm (4-31 Oct) 9.30am-4pm Mon-Sat (1 Nov-28 Mar) 11am-4pm Sun. Closed 24-26 Dec and 1 Jan. **01492 592358**.

Plas Mawr, 9.30am-5pm (29 Mar-21 May) 9.30am-6pm (22 May-5 Sept), 9.30am-5pm (6 Sept-3 Oct), 9.30am-4pm (3-31 Oct). Closed Mondays except Bank Holiday Weekends. **01492 580167**.

Segontium Roman Fort, 9.30am-5.30pm Mon-Sat, (Mar, April & Oct). 2pm-5pm Sun. 9.30am-6pm Mon-Sat (1 May-30 Sept). 2pm-6pm Sun. 9.30am-4pm Mon-Sat (1 Nov-28 Feb) 2pm-4pm Sun. Closed 24-26 Dec and 1 Jan. **01286 675625**.

Caernarfon Castle, 9.30am-5pm (29 Mar-21 May) 9.30am-6pm (22 May-3 Oct) 9.30am-5pm (4-31 Oct) 9.30am-4pm Mon-Sat (1 Nov-28 Mar) 11am-4pm Sun. **01286 677617**.

Criccieth Castle, 10am-6pm (29 Mar-26 Sept) Winter closed. **01766 522227**.

Dolwyddelan Castle, open daily 9.30am-6.30pm (Apr-Oct) 9.30am-4pm Mon-Sat (Oct-Mar). 11am-4pm Sun. Closed 25 Dec. **01690 750366**.

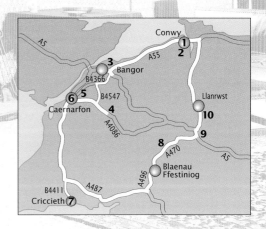

Dunluce Castle.

The MacDonnells –

ADVENTURES IN ANTRIM

**Length: 75 to 150 miles,
one or two days**

**Starting point: Dunluce Castle half
way between Portrush and Bushmills**

An enjoyable holiday of golden
beaches, Giant's Causeway and
Bushmills' whiskey is an essential part
of a tour of the north. Wherever you go
however, you will be near one of the
MacDonnell clan's many triumphs and
disasters.

All the MacDonnell castles and
churches are on the A2 coast road.
Start at **Dunluce Castle** ❶, for a
guided tour, which introduces you to the
amazing wild family, originally an offshoot
of the Scottish MacDonalds, who fought
with and against their neighbours, the
O'Cahans and the O'Neills. Audio guides
are available in several languages. Dunluce
Castle ruins look magnificent on top of dark
rocks. Dating mostly from the 16th and

17th centuries, it was a palace developed
for comfortable living. Its gatehouse looks
Scottish, its Great Hall looks English, and its
kitchen court can boast of numerous
banquets presented to the 2nd Earl, Randall
MacDonnell, who married the Duchess of
Buckingham, Catherine Manners, a lady
who missed London court and hated the
sound of the sea.

Ten miles east on the A2 coast road is
Kinbane Castle ❷ the earliest known of
the MacDonnell castles, built by Colla, who
married local girl Eveleen McQuillan in the
early 16th century. The castle is very small,
but its beauty is its position, a black castle
on a white chalk rock on a golden beach.
Colla's younger brother, Sorley Boy
MacDonnell preferred Ballycastle as his
home, five miles east, along on the coast
road. From here you can see Rathlin Island
and Scotland, and people from this area
travel frequently between Antrim and
Scotland.

The substantial ruins of **Bonamargy
Friary** ❸ in the golf course east of
Ballycastle centre are also 16th and 17th
century. This Franciscan Friary, under the
protection of the MacDonnells, remained
open beyond Henry VIII's dissolution of the

monasteries until the mid 17th century and many of the MacDonnells are buried here. The later graveyard, with pockets reserved for men lost at sea, has many interesting stones. Twenty miles on, travelling first east and then south on the A2 is Cushendall. There the roofless parish church, **Layd Church** ④, built of brown and pink stone beside a stream, is a pretty sight, and has about a dozen interesting gravestones, many of them MacDonnells, all with stories to tell.

Travelling on south along the coast road, you can see two privately-owned castles, **Red Bay Castle** ⑤ immediately south of Cushendall, and visible from the road is very Scottish in character. Twelve miles south is **Glenarm Castle** ⑥ where the current Earl of Antrim, Viscount Dunluce, still lives. From Glenarm, you could return to the start by taking the A42 to Ballymena and the A26 back to the north coast. If you are heading on to Belfast however, stay on the A2 coast road to **Carrickfergus Castle** ⑦ where the second Earl, Randal MacDonnell was twice held prisoner and twice escaped. The castle, which was started in about 1178 has never been unoccupied. It might need a separate day for a serious visit because you need at least an hour to see everything.

For those staying on the north coast and heading west the next day, 30 miles west is Londonderry. The third earl, Alexander MacDonnell, was sent in January 1689 to hold the city for King James II. The gates of **the city walls** ⑧ were slammed in his face, and he and his men fled, pursued by cannon fire. The walls – and the cannon are still there.

OPENING TIMES

Dunluce Castle, 10am-7pm (April-Sept), Mon-Sat, 2pm-7pm Sun.
10am-4pm Tue-Sat (Oct-March), 2pm-4pm Sun.
(028) 2073 1938.

Carrickfergus Castle, 10am-6pm (April-Sept), Mon-Sat, 2pm-6pm Sun.
10am-4pm Mon-Sat (Oct-March). 2pm-4pm Sun.
(028) 9336 5190.

All other sites, free open access.

Above: The City Walls of Londonderry.
Background: Bonamargy Friary.

Following
ST PATRICK

Length: 120 miles on day one, 130 miles on day two, two days or more.

Starting point: Armagh city

Irish missionaries spread all over Europe, Columba to Iona, Columbanus and Fursa to France, Killian to Bavaria, Vergil to Salzburg and many more. This trail follows the tradition of St Patrick with early Irish monasteries, round towers, stone crosses and holy wells all in beautiful landscape settings.

Above: Devenish.
Background: Nendrum Monastery.
Right: Donaghmore Cross.

St Patrick built two churches in **Armagh** ① in the fifth century. The city is the ecclesiastical capital of Ireland with two cathedrals, both dedicated to St Patrick, and is worth a day to itself. Starting with **Navan Fort** ②, the pre-Christian capital of Ulster, two miles west of the city on the A28, the Museum on the Mall provides a general overview of history and St Patrick's Trian is an exhibition which concentrates on the history of the church. On the first day, head east on the A3, to the M1, take exit seven for Hillsborough, and continue to Comber on the A178. **Nendrum Monastery** ③ is signposted

from the A22 south. A winding road takes you island hopping to Mahee Island where St Patrick met Mochaoi and told him to found a church there. What survives is the best example of an early monastery in Northern Ireland, beautifully sited in Strangford Lough. We can still see the three rings of the cashels – stone walls separating the functions of the monastery – and in the visitor centre, a small exhibition explains the details of its life, enhanced by extensive excavation.

Return to the A22 and turn left to **Downpatrick** ④. In the cathedral graveyard is a memorial stone at his traditional burial place and a large 10th-century granite cross with scenes from Old and New Testament on it. At the museum in English Street, close to the cathedral, a small display about nearby sites, including **Struell Wells** ⑤ off the B1 to Ardglass, healing wells in a rocky valley and **Saul Church** ⑥ and **Raholp Church** ⑦, both tiny churches off the A25 to Strangford and both early church sites associated with St Patrick. For those willing to spend longer in the area, **St John's Point Church** ⑧, reached from the B126 from Downpatrick to Killough, is a beautiful example of a small early Irish church. From Killough, you can pick up the A2 coast road, or if you are still at Downpatrick, the A25 to Clough and

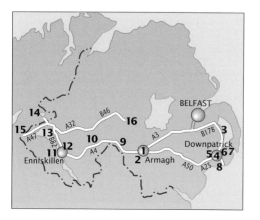

Castlewellan, the A50 to Banbridge, Tandragee and A51 to Armagh.

The second day, leave Armagh on the A28 west, past Navan Fort. Eight miles out, go south to **Tynan** 9 on the B28 to see a stone cross with a carving of Adam and Eve on it. Then go back to the A28 to Augher, left on to the A4 to **Clogher** 10 . Park in the public carpark east of the cathedral and walk into the graveyard. The cathedral is dedicated to St MacCartan, traditionally St Patrick's champion. In the graveyard are two stone crosses, and in the porch a fine early sundial. Behind the church is an earthwork fort, covered in beech trees, multi-period including Early Christian.

Drive straight to **Enniskillen** 11 which stands strategically where the Upper and Lower Lough Erne meet. There are many Early Christian sites around the lakes and pilgrimages going back to at least medieval times led along the waterways, through the Erne system to Lough Derg, where pilgrims still go to an island known as St Patrick's Purgatory. At Enniskillen Castle Museum, a small exhibition describes the pilgrim route and the attractive features still to be seen, especially on Devenish. A good holiday excursion can be to hire a residential motor boat and explore the whole Shannon – Erne waterway. For this day however, follow the A35 Omagh road and take a sharp left down a steep rough drive (signposted) to the **Devenish** 12 ferry. The boat will come from the island on the hour and special arrangements can be made for groups. Devenish is a beautiful sight as you approach by boat. The monastery was founded in the sixth century, and earthworks date back to that time. All the stone buildings are later (12th to 15th centuries), and comprise three churches, a round tower and a stone cross. A small exhibition explains its history. The boat will return you to the shore when you are ready. Drive up the lane and take the B82 left at the top. At Castle Archdale Country Park, the ferry for **White Island** 13 leaves every hour on the hour from the

OPENING TIMES

Navan Centre, daily 10am-5pm. Monument free and open at all times. **(028) 3752 5550.**

Enniskillen Castle, 10am-5pm Mon-Sat, **(028) 6632 5000.**

Devenish Ferry, 10am-6pm (May-Sept), Tue-Sat. 2pm-6pm, Sunday. Hourly on the hour, other times by arrangement. **(028) 9054 3037.**

White Island Ferry, on the hour 10am-5pm, July - August **(028) 6862 1333.**

Belleek Visitor Centre **(028) 6865 8501.**

marina. A 15-minute boat trip brings you to the Island and the 12th-century church is close to the jetty. Inside is a row of fascinating stone figures, in excellent condition that are thought to have come from an earlier church.

If you have time, complete the pilgrimage by driving north to Kesh and Pettigo on the A35 and north on the B233 to the shore of Lough Derg for a view of **St Patrick's Purgatory** 14 . The buildings there today are modern, but the pilgrimage has a long history. For those staying in the area, next stop is to return to Pettigo and turn right on the B136 and A47 to **Belleek** 15 whose famous pottery has its own museum, show-room and café. The pottery's trademark includes a Devenish Round Tower, a hound and a harp. Otherwise turn left at Pettigo on the A35 and return via Kesh, Irvinestown, then the A32 and B46 to Fintona and Clogher. The A4 to Dungannon offers at least one more diversion north for five miles on the A45 and B43 to **Donaghmore** 16 , to see a particularly fine stone cross in the middle of the village. Return to Armagh on the A49 through Moy.

Treat your feet

These rugged, all terrain hiking boots are just what you need to walk your time trail. Our extremely comfortable unisex hiking boots cost just £29.95, including delivery. Lightweight with chunky cleated soles, the boots also feature contoured inner soles for added comfort. They are available in either grey suede with blue panels, or brown suede with green panels, and in all sizes from 4 to 11 inclusive.

To order yours, simply phone the credit card hotline on **01509 638624** or write to us at the address below, enclosing your cheque made payable to RT offers. Please allow 14 days for delivery.

Offer open until 31.12.2000

RADIO TIMES HIKING BOOTS OFFER
(REF.TT01)
BELTON ROAD WEST
LOUGHBOROUGH
LE11 5XL.

ENGLISH HERITAGE

JOIN ENGLISH HERITAGE TODAY

Especially for Radio Times readers:

Join English Heritage and get 15 months' membership for the price of 12

Medieval castles...magnificent houses...enchanting gardens...
English Heritage offers you all the richness of our unique past, with
so many glorious places to visit.

**Join today by direct debit and you can receive 15 months'
membership for the price of 12 months.**

As a member of English Heritage, you can enjoy all this:

* Free access to over 400 treasured sites, from Stonehenge to Hadrian's Wall.

* Free or reduced price entry to regular English Heritage events, including
concerts and special events.

* Free handbook and property map showing all our sites.

* Free copies of our quarterly magazine, Heritage Today.

* The chance to contribute towards preserving our rich national heritage.

Enjoy an extra 3 months **FREE** on all levels of membership.
Your 15 months' for the price of 12 offer applies to all membership levels
shown below:

Membership Type	Annual Fee*
Single adult	£26.00
Single senior citizen	£16.25
Two adults	£42.50
Two senior citizens	£27.50
Family	£45.50

*The membership prices quoted are correct at November 1999 but may change.

What to do now:

All you have to do is sign up for Direct Debit and a year's membership will give you 15
months' free admission to every English Heritage location throughout the country, plus all
the other benefits.

To claim your 15 months' for the price of 12, and to find out more about English Heritage:
* phone us on **01793 414910** quoting reference 6584
* or write to us at: English Heritage, Freepost WD214, PO Box 570, Swindon, SN2 2UR

This offer is available until 31st December 2000

ENGLISH HERITAGE

English Heritage wants to make sure you can continue to enjoy your rich and varied past, which is why we are constantly striving to ensure your history has a future.

Our work includes:

– supporting 365,000 listed buildings, 17,250 ancient monuments and 9000 conservation areas

– identifying other important buildings and monuments for protective listing

– giving conservation grants to churches and cathedrals

– protecting archaeological sites, especially those threatened by developers

– advising the Heritage Lottery Fund on which historic buildings and monuments to support through their grants

– restoring important buildings at risk

– encouraging schools, visitors and the wider public to enjoy England's heritage

– running the Blue Plaques programme in London to show you the houses of famous cultural figures.

Underlying all this work, English Heritage wants to make sure that your history is not only saved, but brought back to life.

2 for 1 Entry to English Heritage sites

2 for 1 entry at Kenilworth Castle, Warwickshire

This voucher entitles the holder to one free entry to Kenilworth Castle, when accompanied by one other paying adult.

Opening times: 1 April - 30 Sept 10am - 6pm daily;
1 Oct - 31 Oct 10am - 5pm daily;
1 Nov - 31 March 10am - 4pm daily

2 for 1 entry at Pevensey Castle, Sussex

This voucher entitles the holder to one free entry to Pevensey Castle, when accompanied by one other paying adult.

Opening times: 1 April - 30 Sept 10am - 6pm daily;
1 Oct - 31 Oct 10am - 5pm daily;
1 Nov - 31 March 10am - 4pm Wed - Sun

2 for 1 entry at Goodrich Castle, Herefordshire

This voucher entitles the holder to one free entry to Goodrich Castle, when accompanied by one other paying adult.

Opening times: 1 April - 30 Sept 10am - 6pm daily;
1 Oct - 31 Oct 10am - 5pm daily;
1 Nov - 31 March 10am - 4pm daily

2 for 1 entry at Dunstanburgh Castle, Northumberland

This voucher entitles the holder to one free entry to Dunstanburgh Castle, when accompanied by one other paying adult.

Opening times: 1 April - 30 Sept 10am - 6pm daily;
1 Oct - 31 Oct 10am - 5pm daily;
1 Nov - 31 March 10am - 4pm Wed - Sun

2 for 1 entry at Pendennis Castle, Cornwall

This voucher entitles the holder to one free entry to Pendennis Castle, when accompanied by one other paying adult.

Opening times: 1 April - 30 June 10am - 6pm daily;
1 July - 31 Aug 9am - 6pm daily; 1 Sep - 30 Sep 10am - 6pm daily; 1 Oct - 31 Oct 10am - 5pm daily;
1 Nov - 31 March 10am - 4pm daily

2 for 1 entry at Brodsworth Hall, S Yorkshire

This voucher entitles the holder to one free entry to Brodsworth Hall, when accompanied by one other paying adult.

Opening times - House: 1 April - 31 Oct 1pm - 6pm Tues - Sun & Bank Hols; Gardens, tearoom, shop and servant's wing: 1 April - 31 Oct noon - 6pm daily;
1 Nov - 26 March 11am - 4pm weekends only

2 for 1 entry at Audley End House/Gdns, Essex

This voucher entitles the holder to one free entry to Audley End House & Gardens, when accompanied by one other paying adult.

Opening times: 1 April - 30 Sept 11am - 6pm Wed - Sun & bank holidays; 1 Oct - 31 Oct 10am - 3pm Wed - Sun;
1 Nov - 31 March Closed

2 for 1 entry at Ranger's House, London

This voucher entitles the holder to one free entry to Ranger's House, when accompanied by one other paying adult.

Opening times: 1 April - 30 Sept 10am - 6pm daily;
1 Oct - 31 Oct 10am - 5pm daily;
1 Nov - 31 March 10am - 4pm Wed - Sun

Index of historic sites